Educate & Rejuvenate

A Three-Step Guide to Revitalize Your Teaching, Renew Your Spirit, and Reignite Your Passion For Life

Kelsey Sorenson

Educate & Rejuvenate

© 2024 by Kelsey Sorenson

All rights reserved. No part of this publication may be reproduced in any form or by any means—electronic, photocopying, recording, or mechanical means, including information storage and retrieval systems without permission in writing from the publisher, except by a reviewer who may quote brief passages in a review. For more information regarding permission, contact the publisher at publishing@teachergoals.com. For bulk purchases go to teachergoals.com/bulk.

Published by TeacherGoals Publishing, LLC Beech Grove, IN
www.teachergoals.com
Cover Design by: Tricia Fuglestad
Interior Design by: Heather Brown and Aubrey Labitigan
Edited by: Dr. John Wick, Ed.D., Carrie Turner, and Kate Allyson

Library of Congress Control Number: 2024940003
Paperback ISBN: 978-1-959419-24-2
ASIN: B0D4N2JCP7

First Printing September 2024

Dedication

To Parker, Brielle, and Peter, I am lucky to be both your mom and your teacher. And to my husband, Randy Sorenson, for sharing this parenting and teaching journey with me. Love you, babe.

Disclaimer

This book is not a replacement for mental health support. At times, professional support is necessary. If at any point you find emotions overbearing and the tools in this book aren't enough, be sure to reach out to a mental healthcare professional for additional support.

Some of the stories in this book are true stories. For those ones, all names and identifying details have been changed. Other stories are fictional but based in patterns I have seen play out in various coaching settings.

Table of Contents

Introduction 1

Chapter 1: Get Curious (Like a Student Teacher) 9

Chapter 2: Is It Really True? (You Don't Have To Believe Every Thought You Think!) 19

Chapter 3: The Self-Coaching Model That Changed My Life 39

Chapter 4: Understanding Our Feelings 57

Chapter 5: Befriending Our Nervous System 71

Chapter 6: Taking Back Your Power of Choice 89

Chapter 7: The Power of Conscious Thinking 107

Chapter 8: Choosing Your Dreams & Goals 123

Chapter 9: Getting Aligned with Your Direction 141

Chapter 10: Intentional Scheduling 157

Chapter 11: Embracing The Educate & Rejuvenate Journey 173

Conclusion Your Educate & Rejuvenate Transformation Begins Now 189

Acknowledgements 195

Bibliography 201

Introduction

"Ugly crying" on my classroom floor as a 22-year-old student teacher was far from my proudest moment. You'd think that one of my third graders would be the one crying over a lost library book, not me.

The emotions I had bottled up were coming out through uncontrollable sobs. I was so consumed in my own despair that I hardly noticed the chaos I had created in my frantic search for the lost book, with scattered papers and belongings strewn across the floor. It didn't register that it was getting dark outside my classroom window and that my husband had probably wondered why he hadn't heard from me yet, long after the school bell had signaled the end of the day.

I was so lost in my sobs that I was unaware that my sweet mentor teacher was trying to console me. Instead, I prayed that the sound of my cries would drown out the voice in my head telling me, *"If you can't even keep track of a library book... how will you ever be a successful teacher?"* Crumpled on the carpet, it became painfully clear that it wasn't the book that brought me to tears—it was the weight of my insecurities and inadequacies suffocating me with every breath.

The school I was student teaching at was in a low-income area. My students faced a variety of problems at home: lack of resources, hygiene issues, and even incarcerated parents.

Many of these students struggled to focus and stay awake. They were not eager to learn. I made it my mission to ignite their passions through student-led learning. When it was time to teach about animals and their habitats, I decided to do a group project. Each group would show off their hard work to the class with a

"Habitat Fair" at the end of the unit, where they'd be the experts and tell everyone who stopped by their exhibit about the habitat and their assigned animals within them.

As I explained the unit, I could see the student's eyes light up. They were finally excited about something! I wanted to encourage their excitement by ensuring they had the materials necessary to succeed and easily find the information they needed, but there was a problem. The books at the school library were insufficient for them to get the information they needed. With no iPads and only two ancient computers for the entire class, technology was not the answer either.

So, I went to the public library and checked out every habitat book I could get my hands on, on my library card, for the kids to research.

However, after the unit ended and I needed to collect all the books to return them to the public library, one of them was missing. In hindsight, I am amazed that only *one* book was gone... but as a naive new teacher, the thought that a book would go missing hadn't even crossed my mind. I hadn't kept track of who had which book. I searched their desks and the classroom. I asked the students if they had an extra book at home by chance. No response. I found myself empty-handed. After a fruitless search for the book inside my students' desks, I knew for sure that it was gone for good— and I was responsible for ensuring its safe return. Hence my breakdown on the classroom floor where I found myself in that dramatized, snotty mess.

You might think that this toddler-esque meltdown was a bit of an overreaction, but all of these tears and heartache were not simply over a lost library book. I had hit a breaking point.

Through the stress of student teaching, preparing for a new baby (who would be arriving in just a few months), and our finances now that I'd left my job to student teach, I had been resisting the emotions and bottling them up carefully. This was the moment that the metaphorical bottle exploded.

Over the years of working with educators, I've realized I'm far from alone in this experience. Many educators are reaching their limits. Simply pull up an education news article, and you'll find that teacher burnout is at an all-time high. According to a 2022 Gallup panel, 44% of educators said they were burned out "always" or "very often," outpacing all other industries nationally (Marken & Agrawal, 2022). The most common feeling that comes up with my clients in coaching sessions is "overwhelmed."

These feelings of stress are also apparent when you look at the deeper messages in teacher memes on social media. From the popular graphic comparing teaching to taming velociraptors in Jurassic Park to the numerous memes about there not being enough coffee to get through the day–what do these have in common? They make us laugh so we don't cry about our struggles.

When we live in a consistent state of overwhelm and neglecting our needs, we may feel like we are just surviving with the demands of being an educator. Between the widening gaps in education from a global pandemic, substitute shortages, and the many shifts in education, education has become an ever-changing landscape.

Does this mean educators must choose between loathing their lives or quitting teaching? Not necessarily. Despite the odds, there are educators who are thriving, but the playbook has changed. Now, that playbook is in your hands to guide you through this process, starting wherever you are. You can get off the roller coaster when you choose to "Educate & Rejuvenate."

The "Educate & Rejuvenate" movement began when my team and I hosted a virtual conference in 2022. Over the past couple of years, the phrase has resonated deep within the hearts of thousands of educators everywhere. In their own words, attendees said these events have helped them feel "hope, joy, and inspiration" so they could get their fire back. I hope you feel the same experience throughout this book.

I wrote this book for all educators. Whether you teach preschool, elementary, secondary, or adults in a traditional classroom, online, or homeschool your own children, this book will help you thrive as a teacher.

The strategies you'll learn will help you have a healthier relationship with your role as an educator because you'll start incorporating the missing piece: **rejuvenating *yourself*.** And I'm not just talking about taking a bubble bath, getting your nails done, or "fluffy" self-care. Nothing is wrong with that; it can be a part of taking care of yourself. But what is going to make the biggest difference is a deep soul rejuvenation, allowing you to:

- Connect with yourself and know your deep needs and desires so you can actually meet them.
- Develop awareness of what is happening inside your mind and body to stop the emotional buildup that leads to constant overwhelm.
- Be able to calm yourself down in the moment when you're feeling stressed so that you can show up the way you want to.
- Stop people pleasing and finally listen to your inner voice to honor yourself while still authentically serving others.
- Navigate boundaries and crucial conversations with coworkers instead of letting resentment fester.
- Cultivate more positive self-talk to feel confidence and joy in teaching and life.
- Learn to be motivated by love instead of fear to live a life of abundance.

Rejuvenating yourself outside of just living and breathing the role of "teacher" will help you provide your life's best work as an educator. You need to show that love for yourself by looking inward before you can impact your students and others in your life in the best way.

Are you ready for a soul rejuvenation that begins from within? I am here to help you discover how to thrive inside and outside of teaching. I can help you because I "get" you. While I've taught in the classroom and homeschooled my kids, I've supported over 100,000 teachers through my resources and blog over the past ten years.

And now, as a life coach, I hold space for those in our community to navigate whatever challenges are coming their way every week via my coaching program, podcast, and social media community. Our Educate & Rejuvenate community involves all kinds of teachers, including general education teachers, administrators, homeschoolers, SPED teachers, college professors, and others.

I'm far from the only person with a breakdown like the one I had over a library book. From the veteran teacher of over 20 years who felt like a beginner again when switching to a new grade level, to the homeschool mom at her wit's end with her child's unique needs, to the educator who was struggling with weight gain as he found himself heading to the pantry each time he got stressed out, these situations seem to come up for almost every educator.

Through my work as a life coach, I've put together a three-step Educate & Rejuvenate coaching framework:

- **Be The Observer:** In the first five chapters of this book, you will learn how to go from subconsciously being driven by your thoughts and feelings to understanding what is going on with your conscious mind. You'll gain strengths in self-awareness, metacognition (thinking about your thinking), and mindfulness. This first step of the framework is the foundation of this work and will help you understand yourself unlike ever before.
- **Choose Your Direction:** In the book's next three chapters, you'll take your observations and consciously choose what you want to keep and what you want to let go of. You'll become

clear on your desires and become conscious of your thoughts and processing your feelings. And finally, you'll set goals to get you where you want to go.
- **Align Yourself:** The final three chapters of this book will help you choose your direction and stick to your long-term goals. You'll also learn strategies for increasing your comeback rate when you get off track, reassessing your choices, and noticing and celebrating your progress.

Figure I.1
Educate & Rejuvenate Coaching Framework

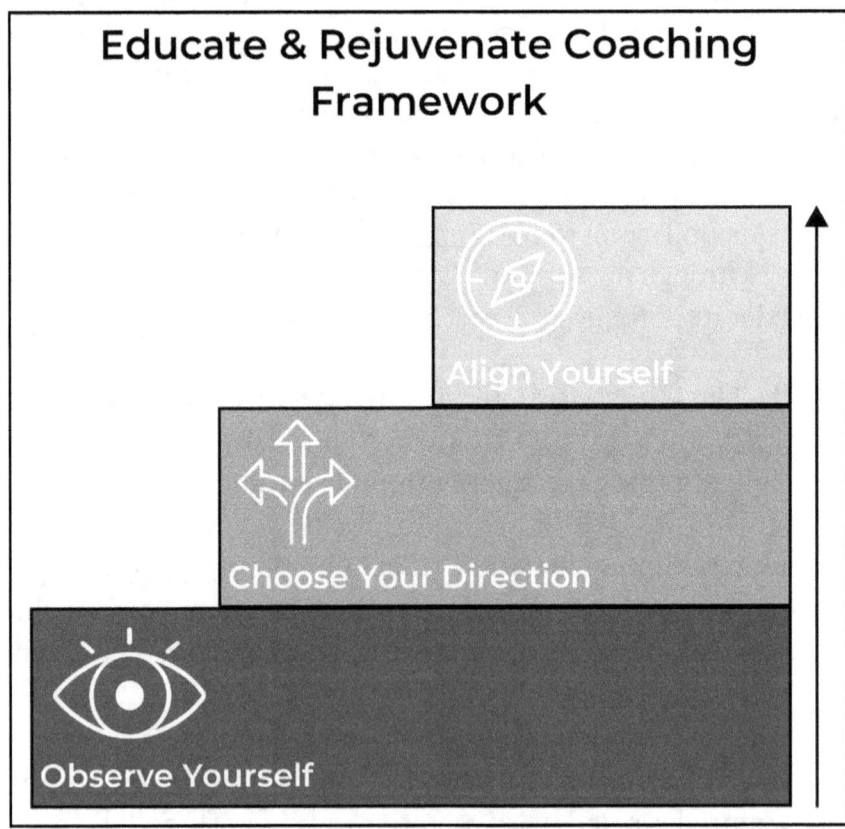

However, this framework isn't just a to-do list to cross off and call it a day. Rather than a one-and-done framework, each step builds upon each other. This book's pages will help you build awareness and create the habits to make "Educating & Rejuvenating" a lifestyle rather than a checklist.

The first step to your Educate & Rejuvenate transformation is to commit to reading and finishing the book. Even if that is all you do, you'll see shifts in your mindset and perspective because you can't "unknow" the tools or any a-ha moments you have while reading.

However, the most significant transformation comes with reading and applying the strategies taught in this book. You'll notice shifts as soon as you apply these tools. We have had community members who have used these tools for just a few months and have seen a huge difference. As you start implementing, you'll feel greater self-love and appreciation for your life.

You will be in awe if you continue this process for a whole year. The tools you learn in this book and the exercises in the free workbook (www.teachergoals.com/educate-resources) will help you to change your direction, make taking intentional action more effortless, and transform your life. Your relationships will take on new meaning as you learn how to stop people-pleasing and live more authentically.

An *Educate & Rejuvenate* lifestyle is a process, not a destination. We never "arrive" at some destination where our lives are perfect. Even as I write this, I still find myself overwhelmed sometimes with all my teaching responsibilities. The difference is that I now have the framework and tools to shift that overwhelm and not stay there.

We want to get to some destination because we think that is when we will feel better. But we truly want the feeling we think we will have when we get there. More than anything else, we just want to feel good. I have the best news for you: you can feel that way. **Let's get started!**

Step One: Observe Yourself

Normally, we just go with the flow of our lives. We don't take the time to notice what we're thinking, feeling, or experiencing. Our brain sees problems outside of us and naturally overlooks the solutions that can come from within. When we become observers, we pay attention to the way we think about problems so that we can resolve them from within.

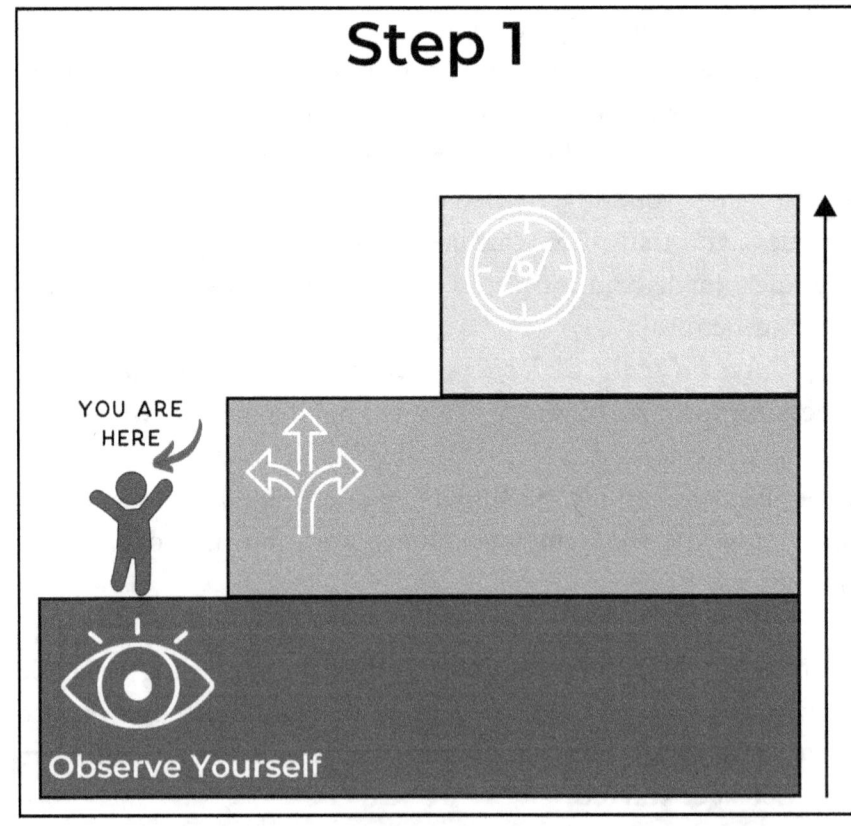

1

Get Curious
(Like a Student Teacher)

Let me guess...you picked up this book because you are ready to change your actions, results, and life, basking in the rejuvenation of it all! After all, that is what was promised, right?

Not so fast, my teacher friend. Now is the time to slow down. This inclination to always be productive, relentlessly striving to go from one thing to the next, is part of the problem.

Most of the teachers, homeschool parents, and administrators I have coached have found themselves stuck in overwhelm. They are doing so many incredible things in their teaching and lives, though they may not realize it. And yet, at the end of the day, they feel drained and unfulfilled. Then they wake up the next day and do it all again.

Take Trina for example, a dedicated single parent juggling a full-time job as a preschool teacher while raising three kids and assisting her sister with her two young nephews. Her days are a whirlwind of work, school pickups, dinner preparations, homework assistance, and managing extracurricular activities. Weekends are filled with chores, errands, family obligations, and volunteer work. With a tight budget due to her middle child's medical needs, Trina spends her evenings coupon hunting to stretch her dollars, often falling asleep while scrolling through her phone for deals.

She explains her situation: "I'm exhausted because I'm just one of those people who does everything for everyone else, and so whatever I need gets put on the back burner."

Does this sound familiar to you? While your exact situation might look different, there's a good chance you have your version of this experience. How often in your day-to-day life do you simply feel sucked into all of the different "hats" you wear? Teacher, parent, grandparent, partner/spouse, neighbor, family member, volunteer… the list goes on and on. You might even move from one role right into the next without giving yourself a chance to stop and breathe.

You, like Trina, aren't doing anything inherently wrong. However, these habits aren't sustainable for your mental, physical, and emotional health if you aren't rejuvenating yourself. When we're in a frantic energy and decide to make changes in our lives, we're setting ourselves up for failure. Whether we know it or not, we're working against our subconscious thoughts and feelings. And if we do nothing, we'll likely keep having the same thoughts and feelings leading to the same results.

So, we will start with a new approach. We will slow down and become observers of ourselves. Life coaching is like tutoring, except the subject you study is yourself.

You already have all the capabilities you need to do this. As educators, we observe our students and their needs, make plans, and adjust as needed. These are skills you have likely already developed. Now, we are going to utilize those same skills on ourselves.

Becoming an observer of ourselves is a practice in both metacognition and mindfulness. Metacognition is when we think about our thinking, and mindfulness is a mental state that we get into when we focus on awareness of the present moment, including our feelings, thoughts, and body sensations.

As you become an observer, you will gain awareness of your thoughts, feelings, and nervous system and how they shape your experiences. You'll learn about the mind-body connection and how it all ties together. As you do this, you'll gain deeper insight into your needs.

You might _believe_ that everything is entirely out of your control because you _feel_ like everything is out of your control. But as you observe yourself, you'll notice where your thoughts might be getting in your way, and that your thoughts are what is causing you to feel out of control. You'll also see the sensations in our body and when you need to take a moment to regulate yourself instead of pushing through. You'll be "slowing down to speed up" by paying attention to these things.

Why We Don't Want to Jump to "Fixing" Things Immediately

Whenever we perceive that something is wrong, we want to fix it. In reality, we might be causing more problems for ourselves by trying to change things before looking at the root cause. That is why the type of coaching I like to use is called "causal coaching," where we get to the root cause of why something is happening before looking for the solutions. It's similar to how a failing grade only indicates a larger picture of what a student needs. The issue will persist until we get to the root cause.

Once, I coached a woman, let's call her Ashley, while teaching a virtual class. Ashely said that she wanted to be able to enjoy the rest of her summer, but she was having a hard time doing that because she was worrying over her to-do list. There were only two and a half weeks left until school started, and she said she wanted to have fun in the summer, but struggled when there wasn't structure. She also had a list of things she wanted to get done, and was worried that she wouldn't accomplish them.

Instead of diving in immediately and asking Ashley about why she didn't get the things done or looking at her schedule to make room for everything, as a life coach, my goal was to get curious about the root cause of the problem for this client. I asked her lots of questions, and she shared that she's the type of person who bases her self-worth on what she gets done. She thrives off of accomplishing everything on her to-do list. This happens frequently with educators, even more so than many other professions. After all, we chose to teach because we have a deep intrinsic drive to help others. The problem for Ashley was that she was telling herself, "I don't have any more time to get these things done," which made her feel anxious.

We realized that when she felt this way, it prevented her from completing what she wanted to do that summer. She was spinning in anxiety instead of getting anything done or giving herself some leisure. She couldn't enjoy her time because she constantly repeated her thoughts about having only two weeks left.

If I tried to tell her to do the things, that wouldn't help. Trying to put a bandage to change what she did without looking at her beliefs and emotions would create resistance that she would be working against, making changing anything over the next two-and-a-half weeks challenging.

As her coach, I decided that the best route was to take a moment to process these emotions since she was feeling such intense waves of anxiety. She was resisting her feelings and trying to push them away. I took her through a quick body scan, where she started at the top of her head, went through the sensations in her body, and observed them. She said this was the first time she'd stopped to consider her feelings.

We discussed what was happening, and I told her nothing was wrong. There was no reason to judge her thoughts and feelings. If she wanted to, she could keep doing what she was doing and continue feeling anxiety rather than checking the things off her list. What mattered most wasn't what was on her list, it was whether she was showing up the way she wanted to in her life. She wanted to see a change because she wanted to feel better.

Now that she had become an observer, I asked her, "What do you truly want these last few weeks of summer?"

"I want to enjoy my summer!"

So I asked her what it meant to her to enjoy her summer. She said it meant doing the things she wanted to do, making progress but not focusing so much on the impending self-imposed deadline and instead letting it be what it is.

As she came to this realization, I saw a clear "lightbulb" moment, just like we see with the kids we teach as educators. Her face softened, and we even got a smile and a laugh as she realized what she really wanted. By the end of the call, Ashley walked away with clarity, feeling hopeful that she could let go of the pressure she'd been putting on herself.

Do you see now why we want to look at the root cause before we attempt to make changes? If we don't know what we're dealing with, we're working against ourselves. Becoming an observer allows us to see what is actually happening that we likely would have never noticed otherwise.

What It Means to Observe Yourself Objectively

When you think of "observing yourself," you might picture yourself with a rubric, grading your performance. You might be ready to write down everything you think you might be doing wrong, and you might already have an idea of how things "should" be going—and that's what you judge yourself against.

However, if we have an agenda, we are not objectively observing ourselves. We want to come into this with as little judgment as possible. We don't want to look at ourselves as a principal evaluating whether or not we are "highly effective," giving scores, or leaving notes on what went well (and what didn't).

Instead, imagine yourself as a student teacher in an education program with fresh eyes. As a pre-service teacher, you know some things about teaching, but there's a lot you have yet to learn simply from observing someone else do it. Imagine that, as this new educator, you're watching an experienced teacher without a checkbox or rubric for what you "should" be seeing. You're coming in with curiosity and wonder.

If the teacher did something you think you would have done differently, you might think, *"Oh! I wonder why she did that. That's interesting. I should look at that a bit closer."* This is the same way we want to approach observing ourselves. We're simply watching and taking notes with fascination.

When I look at the thoughts I'm having, I tell myself, "I'm just studying Kelsey, I want to know what Kelsey is doing." Using third-person language helps remind me that I am observing myself as an outside observer. I'm looking to see what's factually happening rather than seeing if I've been doing what I want to have been doing. I might also ask myself, "What is she thinking? How is she feeling? What does that feel like in her body?" Figuratively speaking, I'm just here to enjoy the show, as if I'm at the next big blockbuster with a large bucket of popcorn and a Diet Coke.

Tap Into Self-Compassion Instead of Judgement

As we become observers, we don't want to use the tools we

learn in this book to judge or shame ourselves. But we are human, so we want to notice when this inevitably happens.

When we judge ourselves for what we see, we simply add layers of shame and judgment on top of the situation. Having a negative thought about having a negative thought won't help us solve any problems. While we start our observations with curiosity and fascination, it is human nature that some judgment will also pop up occasionally. As soon as we notice judgment emerge, we want to tap into self-compassion, just like we would do with our students. Most educators have found that utilizing positive reinforcements and kindness helps us with behavior management, much more so than coming down on our students in anger. If our students deserve this, we do as well!

In the book *Self Compassion*, Dr. Kristin Neff shares what her studies have shown to be the three core components of self-compassion (Neff, 2011, pp. 41-42):

1) Self-kindness: being gentle and understanding with ourselves rather than being critical. We can recognize that we deserve just as much love as any other human.

When you think critically about yourself, especially as you start observing your thoughts, ask yourself, "Would you say that to one of your students or your children?" If not, remember: you also used to be a little child. And in the case of learning these tools, you *are* the student studying yourself. We want to notice when we say things to ourselves that we wouldn't say to any other student who is learning a new skill.

2) Recognize our shared humanity: we want to feel that our experiences connect us with humanity and that our suffering doesn't alienate us. Everyone suffers from time to time.

3) Mindfulness: we hold our experience in awareness rather than ignoring the pain altogether or blowing it out of proportion. Notice how this ties into the "being an observer" concept.

Not only has self-compassion been well-researched and pioneered by Dr. Neff, but wisdom traditions and religions worldwide also teach the importance of love and compassion. From the Buddhist perspective, you have to care about yourself before you care about others, because we are all one. We are interconnected, and if you try to love those around you while treating yourself worse than others, you're creating a divide between yourself and everyone else. Similarly, Sikhism promotes love and compassion for all beings. The concept of "Sarbat da Bhala" translates to the well-being of all and reflects a commitment to the welfare of the entire human race.

In the Bible, Jesus also taught his followers to "love thy neighbor as thyself." While many interpret this to mean that we need to love others, we also need to look at it the other way around. The way we love ourselves is the way we love others. How we think impacts how we feel, which affects what we do. If we have feelings other than love towards ourselves, that energy will follow us into other relationships. We want to give ourselves the same grace we give the students we teach.

Part of your journey throughout the book will be about loving and accepting yourself as you are. As you observe yourself, look for the reasons to love yourself. Even as you notice parts you want to change, know that if you choose to change anything, you're making that choice out of self-love.

Self Awareness Is the Key

By becoming an observer, you are becoming self-aware. Self-awareness is the key that unlocks the potential for all of the other tools presented in this book. For this reason, these first five chapters are the most important ones. We can't do the remaining steps of the book without first learning how to observe ourselves.

To start, get a baseline of where you are. Try the following exercise. Pick a period of 24 hours to start observing yourself (you could start right now or tomorrow morning, but make it soon). During this time, you will become an observer. Tap into being that student teacher watching yourself. Have a notebook nearby, or even utilize the notes app on your phone to make it easy.

Watch for:
- How you treat yourself,
- Your self-talk,
- The emotions you feel throughout the day, and which emotions you feel the most often,
- What you do when you get overwhelmed,
- How you feel in your body.

Whenever you get a chance, write down what you notice. Don't overthink it or edit yourself. You're the only one who will see it, so just write it down.

As you do this, don't try to fix anything right away. Remember, the first step is self-awareness, which is powerful, so we want to stay there for a moment. But if you notice an urge to fix something, I want you to see that, too. Then, lovingly bring yourself back to being a compassionate, curious observer of yourself.

After you've completed your initial observation of yourself, I want you to journal your answers to the following questions:

- How self-aware do you think you have been up to this moment?
- Do you find that you come from a place of judgment or curiosity while observing yourself? Give an example.
- Did you find yourself jumping to "fix" problems as you're observing?
- What are some things that you noticed that surprised you?

SCAN THE QR CODE or go to www.teachergoals.com/educate-resources for your printable Educate & Rejuvenate workbook featuring these questions and more!

2

Is It Really True?
(You Don't Have to Believe Every Thought You Think!)

"Between stimulus and response, there is a space. In that space is our power to choose our response. In our response lies our growth and our freedom." While the true origins of this quote are unknown, Viktor Frankl has often been attributed to this quote that mirrors his experiences (Schorling, 2024).

Imprisoned in Nazi concentration camps, Frankl, a psychiatrist, keenly observed the psychological mechanisms at play in himself and his fellow prisoners as they struggled to survive under harsh conditions. His will to survive was supported by a flicker of hope, fueled by thoughts of reuniting with his wife and sharing the lessons learned through adversity as an instructor once he escaped.

Frankl believed that this hope increased his odds of surviving as a prisoner, by using the power of the human spirit to transcend circumstances and find significance in life. He shares,

"Everything can be taken from a man but one thing: the last of the human freedoms—to choose one's attitude in any given set of circumstances, to choose one's own way (Frankl, 2006, p. 66)."

As educators, we have this same power to overcome the challenges we face. While ours may not be as life-threatening or dire as Frankl's experience, the statistics show us that educators frequently find themselves feeling burned out and hopeless. How can we, too, choose hope in the face of adversity?

While we can't always control our external environment, we do have the power to shape our inner landscape—our thoughts. This is where the power of thought work shines; not by denying reality, but by cultivating thoughts that bring us meaning and hope, regardless of circumstance.

What Is Thought Work?

The idea that our thoughts create our feelings and how we show up in the world, known as "thought work," has been contemplated for centuries. For example, Roman Emperor and Stoic Philosopher Marcus Aurelius, whose reign was from 161-180 AD, is often quoted with, "You have power over your mind—not outside events. Realize this, and you will find strength (Augustine, 2024)."

Epictetus, Greek Stoic Philosopher (55–135 AD), also said, "We cannot choose our external circumstances, but we can always choose how we respond to them (Rose, 2024)." And Ralph Waldo Emerson (1803–1882) said, "A man is what he thinks about all day long (Fletcher, 2024)."

In 1970, these ponderings were adapted into a therapeutic approach when Aaron Beck founded cognitive behavioral therapy (CBT) while searching for a treatment for depression. He realized that patients with depression often had distorted thought patterns and that changing the thought patterns alleviated the patient's symptoms. His findings were adapted to apply a wide variety of scenarios and practices. According to Beck, "Cognitive therapy is based on the idea that when you change the way you think, you can change the way you feel and behave (Beck et al., 2024)."

Since the discovery of CBT in 1970, new findings and approaches have emerged for therapists to help patients change their thinking, mood, and behavior. CBT backs the thought work approaches in this book, put into a self-coaching model that makes it accessible for anyone to learn and use.

Observing our thoughts starts by understanding the difference between our thoughts and circumstances. While defining these terms may sound simple and even silly, trust me, we need help identifying the difference!

Our Thoughts, Not Our Circumstances, Create Our Feelings

Our circumstances are simply facts or situations that we don't have control over at this moment. A recent winter trip to California showed me this reality in action. I live in Salt Lake City, Utah, where our snowy winters can reach freezing temperatures. Accustomed to Salt Lake City's freezing winters, I had only packed jeans, and I found the 70-degree weather warm. I wished I had packed shorts. However, my search for shorts proved futile, and I was surprised to see locals donning coats in what I considered beautiful weather.

We were all in the same 70 degrees but had different interpretations of how that felt. While not everyone will agree on the best way to dress for 70-degree weather (our thoughts), we can agree that it is 70 degrees outside (the circumstance).

Circumstances, by themselves, aren't subjective. Because of this, they can be described as "neutral," meaning they are neither good nor bad on their own— they just exist. We must identify the facts because this helps us separate what we can't control from what we can influence.

Our tendency to attribute our feelings to external circumstances is often reflected in our language. Take the statement, "I'm overwhelmed by my to-do list," for example. While it may seem innocuous, it places the blame for the feeling on the to-do list itself. However, different individuals may have varied perspectives on the same list—some may find it manageable, while others might see it as insufficient or excessive. Ultimately, it's our thoughts about the to-do list that drive our feelings.

Even the words you are reading on this page are a circumstance. Some educators might read these words and think, *"This is exactly what I've been looking for,"* and feel excited to improve their lives inside and outside of teaching. Others might think, *"I don't think anything could help me with my levels of burnout,"* and feel discouraged. Even though anyone who picks up this book is reading the same sentences on the page, they may interpret it differently.

As Dr. Judith Beck (a renowned CBT expert who is also the daughter of CBT pioneer Aaron Beck) explains that "the way people feel emotionally and the way they behave are associated with how they interpret and think about a situation. The situation itself does not directly determine how they feel or what they do (Beck, 2020)." Our brains add context to them when the circumstances enter our consciousness with our thoughts and underlying beliefs.

Beck shares how we have beliefs and thoughts on three levels:
- **Core beliefs:** These are our most central ideas about the self, others, and the world. They are so fundamental and deep that we often can't even articulate them. We just see them as the

way things are. These beliefs begin developing from an early age, influenced by genetics, childhood upbringing, and the meaning we put behind our personal experiences.

Examples of core beliefs: *I am good enough to be loved by others; I am morally bad; I am competent and in control; I am powerless.*

- **Intermediate beliefs:** These beliefs make up our overall attitudes, rules, and assumptions. Our core beliefs influence the development of our intermediate beliefs.

  Examples of intermediate beliefs: *Failing is a bad thing; If I make a mistake, people will judge me; If I embrace challenges, I can grow stronger.*

- **Automatic thoughts:** These are the fleeting thoughts that seem to pop into our heads at a superficial level, influenced by our intermediate beliefs. These are situation specific and drive our feelings in the given moment.

  Examples of automatic thoughts: *I'm so stupid for messing up during my lesson; These kids are driving me crazy; I'm excited for the opportunities that await me.*

For the sake of simplicity, through the rest of this book, we will be focusing on our automatic thoughts and our beliefs, combining the intermediate and core beliefs into a single category of "beliefs." Our beliefs, just like our thoughts, are ideas rather than facts. They are learned, which means they can be tested and changed over time. That said, our beliefs give us our "lens" to see the world and interpret our circumstances. Unless questioned, our brains will find evidence that aligns with our current beliefs and dismiss what does not.

Since our beliefs will naturally shape our automatic thoughts and drive our emotions, it's crucial to take time to slow down, bring awareness to our thoughts, and question if what we are thinking is true. While we can't control the circumstances of our lives or even the automatic thoughts that arise, we can look for cognitive distortions in our thinking, become conscious, and decide what we want to do next.

What Are Cognitive Distortions?

In his book *Feeling Great*, CBT expert David Burns, MD., shares how cognitive distortions are a "highly misleading way of thinking about yourself and the world." Cognitive distortions are irrational or biased thought patterns that lead to negative emotions and behavior. He explains that these distorted thoughts are causing us to feel miserable, even though they aren't true (Burns, 2020).

Understanding the most common cognitive distortions makes it easier to identify when our thinking isn't serving us. Pulling from various sources, I've compiled a list of the most prevalent distortions in the educators I've worked with in the past two years and included relatable examples to go with each one:

1) All-or-nothing Thinking sees things in an extreme black-or-white mindset with no middle ground. We are thinking in absolutes; it must be a certain way or not at all. Often, we use this against ourselves when we think we must either be a complete success or a total failure. It can also apply to other areas of life—such as considering a person or organization as all good or all bad. Unable to see shades of gray, we miss the beauty and nuance in ourselves and others.

An educator who worries they will fall behind in their career if they don't attend every professional development training or workshop they're interested in is falling into all-or-nothing thinking. Similarly, an educator who has one bad experience at a school and concludes that it must be a bad school is also engaging in all-or-nothing thinking.

2) Overgeneralization happens when we draw broad, negative conclusions from an isolated event and apply it to everything. The big clue that lets us know we are overgeneralizing is when we use words such as always, never, everything, and nothing.

Imagine a friend is running late to meet you for lunch. You might overgeneralize by thinking, *"Why is everyone always late?"*

Another example might be a homeschooling mom who, after a challenging first day of homeschooling, says, "Homeschooling is a mistake and is not going to work for our family."

3) Mental Filtering occurs when your mind filters out any of the positives (of yourself, your workplace, etc.) and focuses solely on the negative. One of my favorite examples of showing what mental filtering looks like is a viral video from one of my favorite authors, Kristina Kuzmic, who was also a keynote speaker at our recent Educate & Rejuvenate conference (Kristina Kuzmic, 2017).

In her video, she started with two empty oversized glasses. Tons of compliments played in the background, and an M&M dropped inside one of the glasses each time. The glass kept piling full of M&Ms until it was nearly full. And then just one person said, "You're not good enough," and one M&M dropped into the second glass.

Immediately, she pushed over the full glass of M&Ms, which shattered on the floor. She grabbed the nearly empty glass with one M&M representing the single insult, held it close to her chest, and walked away in shame. This is a prime example of mental filtering. When we do this, our brain seeks evidence to confirm what we believe. When our thoughts are negative, we'll filter out the positive.

4) Catastrophizing and magnification is characterized by exaggerating the negatives of the situation. We blow things out of proportion and imagine that our situation is much worse than it is. We focus on the worst possible outcome for any given situation.

For example, if a parent of a six-year-old child is struggling to grasp the concept of reading, they may worry excessively about their child being unable to get a job or go to college, simply because they need additional support for some time.

5) Discounting the positive (minimization or trivializing) is similar to mental filtering, with a slight difference. When we discount the positive, we tell ourselves that any positive qualities, compliments, positive feedback, or successes we've had don't count.

For example, a paraprofessional may tell themselves that even though the Apple Watch gave them 30 "active" minutes for a bustling day of teaching, it doesn't count as exercise because it wasn't an official workout. Or a teacher receives glowing feedback on a teacher observation, but it doesn't mean anything because *"they were just saying that to be nice."*

6) Jumping to conclusions is when we make pessimistic predictions and assume the worst will happen without any evidence to back it up. Jumping to conclusions can also be divided into two categories:

<u>*Mind Reading*</u> is when you believe that you know exactly what someone else is thinking and feeling (usually something negative about yourself) even when there is no evidence.

For example, an educator wants to befriend a fellow teacher. The teacher buys a coffee for some fellow teachers, but not them.

They assume it means she hates them, when in reality, maybe she was just getting them for the teachers next door to her, and there are many other teachers she didn't bring one for, too.

Ironically, mind-reading often leads to social anxiety or shyness, which may cause them to withdraw even more from this fellow teacher, preventing the desired relationship.

Fortune Telling is when we believe something terrible is just around the corner for no good reason. As Dr. Burns says, "It's as if you had a crystal ball that only gives you bad news! (Burns 2020)"

An online teacher has a busy day of virtual classes, and some kids seem unengaged. They can't hear the students speak because they mute themselves when they are supposed to talk, and vice versa. This teacher thinks, *"If today's class was this difficult, the rest of the school year would surely be a disaster! They won't learn anything, and everyone will think I'm an awful instructor."*

7) Emotional reasoning happens when we base our reasoning on our feelings as if our feelings are objective. Examples include *"I feel like a failure, so I am a failure."* If you feel lonely in one situation, you think, *"I have no friends."* If you're jealous of your partner, you may think, *"They must be cheating on me!"*

The cognitive distortion of emotional reasoning prevents us from drawing reasonable conclusions. While we want to get in touch with our emotions, they are not objective guides to reality. As we've learned, our thoughts create our feelings, and our thoughts can be riddled with various cognitive distortions.

8) "Should" statements occur when we criticize ourselves or others using the terms "should," "shouldn't," "musts," "ought to," or "have to." With these statements, we generally have unrealistic, rigid, or ironclad rules considering the specifics of the circumstances.

Some examples of statements like this would be:

- These kids should be further ahead.
- I shouldn't have eaten that
- That person shouldn't be the president.
- We have to do better than this.
- Zoom should automatically mute all my students.

As you can see above, "should" statements can be directed at ourselves, others, and the general world. Even if we use these statements to motivate ourselves or others and remind ourselves of our high standards, it doesn't serve us. Instead, it causes undue pressure and stress. Psychologist Clayton Barbaeu coined famous therapy catchphrase "don't should all over yourself" because of this cognitive distortion (Malkasian, 2022).

9) Unfair comparisons happen when we compare ourselves to others, and we take one small part of our performance or situation and compare it to what we see and interpret from someone else's. These are usually unfair comparisons because we take the worst we see in ourselves and compare it to someone else's highlight reel.

It is evident that this is a problem in the teacher world, as one of the top quotes that we have ever shared on social media states the following:

"Whatever you do, don't compare yourself to other teachers. The truth is, we're all a hot mess. Some of us just hide it better than others."

Figure 2.1
Viral Post from Educate & Rejuvenate

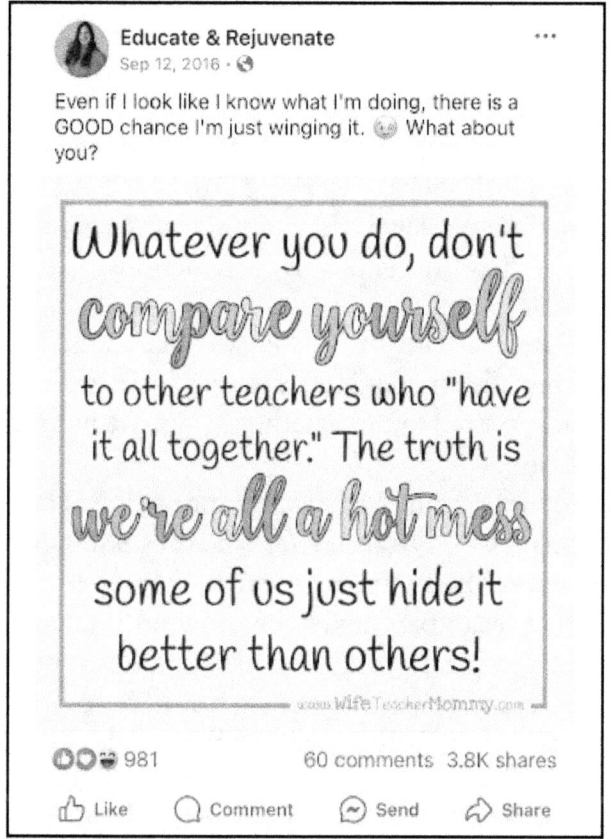

This post resonated with teachers, as it went viral multiple times on our Wife Teacher Mommy social media pages (before we rebranded to Educate & Rejuvenate) with over 3,000 shares. This quote comforted teachers and helped them realize that this comparison isn't fair.

10) Labeling involves attaching negative overall labels to oneself or others based on specific behaviors or mistakes. It's like taking "overgeneralization" and turning it up to the maximum level. You're capturing the essence of yourself or another person with a single label and turning it into an absolute. For example, if someone makes a mistake while teaching a lesson, they might think, *"I'm such an incompetent teacher."* A teacher may also make the mistake of labeling their entire class as "lazy," "unruly," or "disruptive" without taking into account any positive or individual behaviors of members of the class.

A homeschool parent who encounters challenges while balancing homeschooling, working from home, and other responsibilities might label their family as "dysfunctional" or "disorganized," discounting positive interactions.

11) Personalization is when we take excessive blame for situations, especially when it is unwarranted. We believe we are the cause of an adverse outcome, whether or not we have any control over the situation.

An example is when someone's spouse is in a bad mood. If their first thought is, *"What did I do?"* and they assume their spouse is upset because of their actions or words, that is personalization.

Another example might be how a teacher's students performed on a test. They might blame themselves solely for their students' test scores; however, they do not have complete control over that, and they might have done all they could do.

12) Blame is the opposite of personalization. It involves giving full accountability to others for our problems without considering our role or contributions.

One example of this might be working on a group project for a graduate degree. One student doesn't get the grade they were hoping for, and they blame the other group members for it without considering any places where they could have improved their work.

Another example would be if someone is running late for work and blames the unexpected traffic for being late, when really, they also left 15 minutes later than usual.

Understanding these cognitive distortions will help you identify them as they arise as automatic thoughts in your day-today life. Ask yourself: which of these cognitive distortions do I fall into the most often?

Thoughts vs Circumstances in Action

Let's take a look at some sample circumstances and see what some different thoughts might arise. First, I want you to take a look at the chart below. In each example, you can see that the situations in the "circumstance" column are fact-based without any story behind them.

On the "thoughts" side, you'll see potential thoughts someone might have if they were in that situation. As you read each thought, imagine how the person's feelings might change based on their perception. Then, think of another possible thought someone could have about the circumstance.

Figure 2.2
Circumstances and Potential Thoughts

Circumstance	Potential Thoughts
I have a class of 28 third-grade students.	I have a big class. I have a small class. I have the hard class. I have the best class.
The phone rings, and it is your mother-in-law.	What a pleasant surprise! I don't have time for this. Is everything okay?
Lucia has four children.	She has a large family. She has a beautiful family. She has a small family. Lucia has four unruly children.

Soccer begins at 5:30. It's 5:15, and my daughter is looking for her cleats.	I'm always the late mom. We might be right on time. The race is on! I need to add organizing shoes to my list.
I have 32 products listed in my Teachers Pay Teachers (TPT) store, and I've made 54 sales so far.	I need to make more products. My store is a success. No one likes my stuff. I'm on a roll!
The principal said, "I don't think that approach is working. Maybe you should try addressing the issue another way."	That was so rude! I am an awful teacher. She doesn't like me. I wonder why she said that. That's good feedback.

Now, it's time for you to try separating circumstances from thoughts! Below is a list of statements, each a "circumstance" or a "thought." I want you to try reading through these statements and decide if you think it is a "circumstance" or a "thought." (Don't peek at the answers just yet!)

Figure 2.3
Circumstance VS Thought

Statement	Circumstance?	Thought?
I am busy.		
After teaching today, I have two parent meetings.		
I have the worst class.		
They are always late.		

I am 38 years old.		
I always figure it out.		
I am a hot mess.		
My kids never listen to me.		
I have three kids.		
His report card has 3 Fs.		
He should be further ahead by now.		
I teach third grade.		
I can't leave my job.		
Homeschooling is difficult.		
I am an anxious person.		
My teaching contract wasn't renewed.		
I feel like a failure.		
She doesn't like me.		

Let's see how you did!

We will review these statements and label whether it is a circumstance or a thought.

1. ***"I am busy"*** is a thought because it is subjective. An excellent way to know if something is a thought or a circumstance is to ask what it means. One person's "busy" will look like someone else's "normal" day. It's also not always helpful to keep meditating

on the thought, "I am busy," even if you have numerous to-dos on your list. This thought tends to make us feel overwhelmed. There are likely alternate thoughts that could lead you to feel more empowered.

2. *"After teaching today, I have two parent meetings"* is a circumstance. You could pull out your calendar and see that two meetings are scheduled. This circumstance is neutral. However, you might have a thought about it- such as "I am busy," "Today is a productive day," or "I deserve a nap."

3. *"I have the worst class"* is a thought. There is no such thing as a "worst class" or even a "best class." We have a class which is our group of students. Any adjectives that we use to describe the class are our thoughts.

4. *"They are always late"* is a thought, and a prime example of overgeneralization. This is when we apply something that happens one time (or even sometimes) and say it happens every time. The big clue here is that when we use always or never, this isn't true 100% of the time.

5. *"I am 38 years old"* is a circumstance. We could look at a birth certificate and see this person's age.

6. *"I always figure it out"* is a thought. Notice that we used "always" again here, and we could also ask what it means to "figure it out." However, just like any other thoughts on this page, there is nothing wrong with this thought. Depending on whether it resonates with you, this might be a beneficial thought or mantra.

7. *"I am a hot mess"* is a thought. You aren't a mess— you're a person! But this is a pervasive thought we hear people say when they are in overwhelming thinking patterns. Notice how these words aren't valid and could never be true. There's no way for you to change from a person into a "hot mess."

8. ***"My kids never listen to me"*** is a thought. We could ask a group of people, "What does it mean to listen?" and each person would give a different response. We could also question if it is really true. Are there times when they *have* listened? The use of the word "never" is an absolute, which is a signal of the distortion of overgeneralization, as well.

9. ***"I have three kids"*** is a circumstance. You could pull up family pictures or birth certificates to prove you have three children.

10. ***"His report card has 3 Fs"*** is a circumstance. We could pull out the report card and see his grades, and everyone might have different thoughts about what this means.

11. ***"He should be further ahead by now"*** is a thought (and an example of one someone might have about #10). There was a clue with the word "should" that this would fall under a cognitive distortion. Ask yourself, *"How do we know exactly where each child should be?"* You may say, "But they haven't met the benchmarks!" And my question remains the same. What if being "behind" is part of this child's journey? Our job as their teachers is to teach them where they are.

12. ***"I teach third grade"*** is a circumstance, because we could walk into your classroom and see you teach a third-grade class.

13. ***"I can't leave my job"*** is a thought. Leaving your job is always an option. Even if you have a contract, there are ways that you can break the contract. You may not want the consequences, but the key here is understanding that staying in your current position is your choice, and telling yourself otherwise is disempowering. We'll find more options than we considered possible when we stop thinking in absolutes.

14. ***"Homeschooling is difficult"*** is a thought. As we've discussed in many of these scenarios, each of us would describe

"difficult" differently. It probably isn't helping to ruminate on how difficult homeschooling is, either. Rather than that, consider thinking about how you could have more fun while homeschooling. There are as many approaches to homeschooling as there are homeschooling families, so feel free to carve your own path.

15. ***"I am an anxious person"*** is a thought. You are giving yourself a label. Anxiety could be a diagnosis, but even then, this is a label we are putting on ourselves. Just like in the Special Education community, we've been leaning towards not labeling our students by any diagnoses, saying "child with special needs" instead of "special needs child." We don't have to label ourselves as such. It might be what is preventing you from questioning the label in the first place.

16. ***"My teaching contract wasn't renewed"*** is a circumstance. We know this because it is something that we don't have control over, and one could have a variety of thoughts about it.

17. ***"I feel like a failure"*** is a thought. When we say, 'I feel like a failure,' we're delving into emotional reasoning. Essentially, we're allowing our distorted thoughts to dictate our feelings, and then using those feelings to define our reality.

18. ***"She doesn't like me"*** is a thought, highlighting the mind reading cognitive distortion, where we jump to conclusions. This assumption might not hold much truth. We often read too much into situations, focusing on selective evidence while ignoring anything that contradicts our belief. It's like putting on mental blinders, filtering out anything that suggests otherwise.

I'm sure you saw at least a few relatable examples from this exercise. Take a moment to reflect:

- What insights did you gain from doing this exercise and

reading about each statement?
- Do you find yourself frequently thinking any similar thoughts?
- If so, what might you learn about yourself from your observation?

Why Your Current Thinking Makes Sense

There is nothing wrong with the way you are currently thinking. It makes sense, given your current beliefs. As David Burns says in his book *Feeling Great*, "Your negative thoughts and feelings are not, in fact, the result of what's wrong with you... but what's right with you (Burns, 2020)."

Burns explains that our negative thoughts and the corresponding feelings can reveal some beautiful traits about ourselves. Your so-called "negative" thoughts can be a reflection of your core values—and you don't need to change those. As you become more self-aware, you can decide what you want to keep from the new understanding of yourself, and what you want to shift, while still keeping the benefits uncovered.

For example, Sarah is teaching her preschooler how to read. She's been working on CVC words and blending with her son, and they haven't made much progress over the last few months. Sarah thinks, *"I am a terrible teacher. I should have just sent him to preschool!"* and feels deeply ashamed.

What does this thought, and the shame it reveals, tell us about Sarah?
- Her thoughts show that Sarah wants her child to learn how to read
- Teaching her child to read is important to her
- She is observant and has noticed there isn't the progress she was expecting

- Evaluating how she is doing is important to her, and she's willing to humble herself to see if her teaching is working
- Sarah takes her decision to teach her child seriously

As you can see, Sarah's thoughts and feelings aren't telling us anything is wrong with Sarah, but revealing some of the things she truly cares about. However, in the process, she is causing herself pain, and she likely doesn't want to stay there. Once she gains awareness of this, she may also realize that her child's current abilities do not determine her success, but her thoughts and feelings showed that she has perseverance in seeking solutions for her child.

Sarah may realize that she still holds those values of caring about her teaching practices and her child's education, but that she may want to shift to a more solution-focused approach to move forward without shame.

You can do the same thing. While you can't control every thought that enters your mind, you also don't have to believe every thought you think. Observe your thoughts and notice which are distorted. Once you gain awareness, ask yourself, *"Do I really want to believe that?"*

Questioning your thoughts is where your power lies. As Eckhart Tolle, spiritual teacher and self-help author, says, "You are not your thoughts; you are the awareness behind them (Y, 2024)." Remember, your thoughts don't hold authority over you. By assuming the stance of the observer, you unlock the ability to choose which thoughts to accept and which to graciously release.

3

The Self-Coaching Model That Changed My Life

As a child, whenever we learned about something potentially scary in my elementary school class, I'd worry about it happening immediately. For example, after a unit about volcanoes, I sincerely believed that one of the peaks on Utah's Mount Timpanogos was a volcano. Even though my mom assured me this wasn't the case, I feared she was mistaken.

My parents, teachers, and other adults in my life knew about this worrying habit of mine. Well-meaning people would say, "Oh Kelsey, she's a worrier!" Without realizing it, I took on this label of "worrier" as an unchangeable identity trait of myself and never questioned it.

Being self-aware has never come naturally to me; it's been quite the opposite. I would have kept going that way if it weren't for one ER visit five days after the birth of my third child. That panic attack changed the trajectory of my life.

Since we'd arrived home from the hospital after my son's birth, whenever I tried to sleep, my body would "jolt" me awake in panic. I felt a surge like electricity go through me whenever this happened. And unlike my older two children, Peter was an incredible sleeper, so he wasn't keeping me awake. My own body was failing me. It was a scary feeling, so it made me not want to try to sleep, which became a vicious cycle.

Naturally, a lack of sleep led to more severe issues, including the inability to handle my emotions. I lost it not being able to find the TV remote to turn on Cocomelon (a popular kids musical TV show) for my older kids so I could take care of the baby. I didn't even know why, and it terrified me. My breathing patterns were erratic, and the electric jolts continued whenever I tried to sleep. On the third day of experiencing this, I was sure I was having a heart attack.

My husband took me to the emergency room where medical professionals hooked me up to machines, drew my blood, and ran several tests. We spent most of the day in the hospital, and my feelings ranged from panicked *(thought: "They are going to tell me I'm dying")* to embarrassed *(thought: "My husband probably thinks I'm crazy")*.

The hours were painstakingly slow as we awaited the results. Eventually, the doctor assured me that I was not having a heart attack or anything else that was a major physical problem. I was diagnosed with postpartum anxiety.

Given my history of being a chronic worrier, I knew that this diagnosis was only part of what was going on. While I'd reached a breaking point, anxiety was something that affected me long before I ever had children. I knew that returning to my average stability level wasn't enough. I wanted to be in a better mental and emotional place to be available for my family, the educators I worked with, and the team I'd built as my company's needs grew. **I didn't want to be a "worrier" my whole life; I wanted to enjoy my life.**

My doctor prescribed me an antidepressant, and for the first time, I started to see a therapist. Those strategies helped me reach a safer and more stable place, bringing me closer to my original baseline.

A few months later, someone asked me to take on a volunteer responsibility and I didn't feel I could do it. However, prone to people pleasing, I didn't know how to say "no." I posted a desperate plea in a Facebook group, pouring my heart out while sharing the full postpartum story I just shared with you here, and that I felt there was no way I could handle one more responsibility.

Little did I know that one simple Facebook post would change my life. In the comments section, someone suggested I needed to reach out to this girl she knew, Lizzie Langston, a life coach who specialized in working with postpartum women.

I quickly signed up as a client. Lizzie was certified by The Life Coach School, so one of the first tools she taught me was the self-coaching model, which offered a way for me to not only get back to my baseline, but to a better place than ever. I learned how much ownership I could have in all areas of my life: working with kids, having my own family, and running my business supporting teachers and homeschooling parents.

Using the self-coaching model has become a natural habit in my daily life. I realize how my thoughts drive my feelings, actions, and results. I'm not perfect (and never will be), but this tool has given me the power to become self-aware and take back control of my life.

Introduction to The Self-Coaching Model

This self-coaching model was penned by Brooke Castillo, one of my mentors and the founder of The Life Coach School and the top-ranking podcast of the same name (Castillo, 2014).

It is a simple way for anyone to understand the basic concepts of thought work.

This simple yet powerful framework can help us understand how the world works. Members inside the Educate & Rejuvenate Club have incredible breakthroughs when they utilize this concept.

As we learned in Chapter Two, our circumstances are neutral, so we want to separate our circumstances and thoughts. Using the model, we take it a step further as we observe how our thoughts (*not* our circumstances) create our feelings, our feelings drive us to take specific actions (and not others), and our actions produce the results in our lives.

The five parts of the self-coaching model are:
- **Circumstances:** The observable, neutral facts.
- **Thoughts:** The sentences in our mind that make meaning behind the circumstances.
- **Feelings:** The emotion that arises when we have a thought
- **Actions:** The things we do (or don't do) when feeling that way.
- **Results:** What happens when we do or don't do specific actions.

Picture the model like this:

(Image on next page)

Figure 3.1
The Model

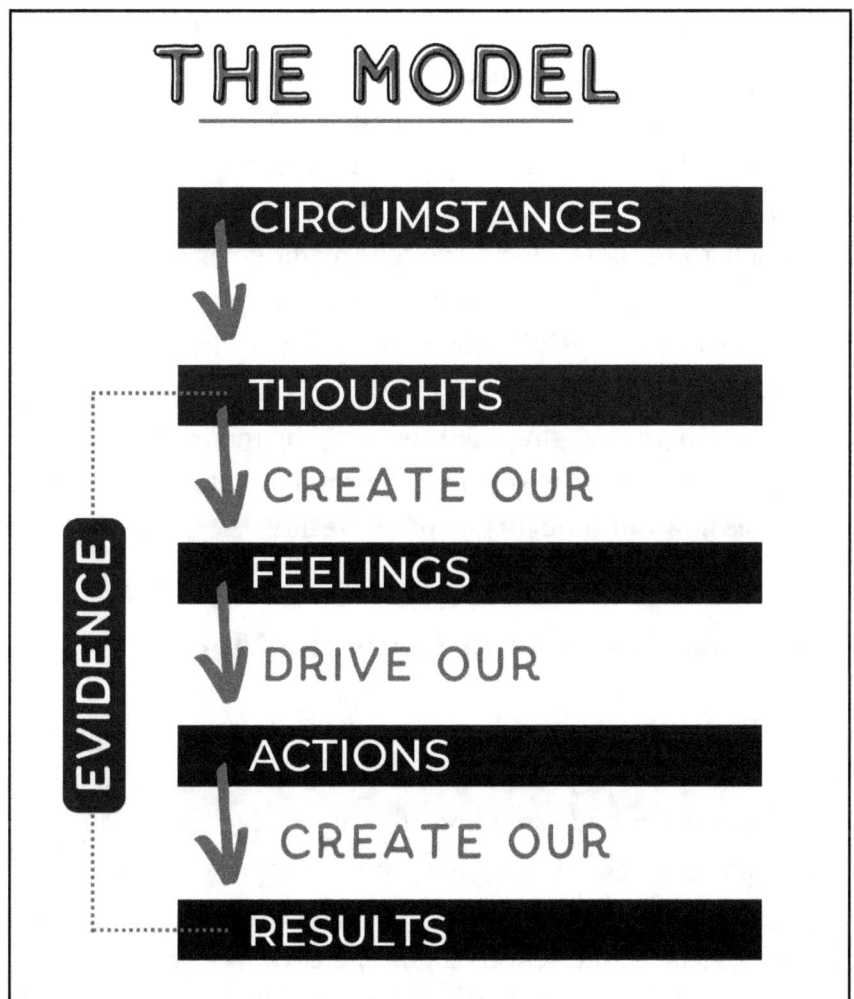

This model is always at work, whether we recognize it or not. Once we can utilize and master this tool, it is game-changing. You'll become more aware of what you're thinking, how it's causing your feelings, what you do (and maybe what you're *not* currently doing), and how that impacts the results you see in your life.

In the image above, an arrow directs your result back to

your thought. That's there for a reason. When you begin grasping the model, you'll see how your thinking directly correlates with the rest of the model (feelings, actions, and results), and that's where the magic happens. You can change...if you want to. The choice is yours!

Sometimes we will want to change, and occasionally we might not. As we discussed in our last chapters, our thoughts are driven by our beliefs, some of which might be positive and important to us. Changing a thought might go against our core values, and we want to feel that way about something!

For example, while advocating for a student, you might like to keep your thought that they aren't getting the support they need rather than changing the thought. The model is not a tool telling us we always have to change our thoughts; it is an awareness tool to see how our thoughts shape our reality.

Stories & Examples of Using the Model

While the self-coaching model's components might be simple, it is a concept you must see in action to start understanding it. Deepening our understanding of it can be a lifelong work. That is why many coaches, therapists, and researchers dedicate their whole careers to understanding the model, CBT, and how our thoughts, feelings, and actions align. There is always more to learn.

Let's start with the basics and some realistic scenarios. I will share some stories below, in these fictional character's words. While these people may be fictional, they are based on a combination of authentic experiences. As you read each story, I want you to identify the parts of the self-coaching model. Specifically, what are their thoughts, and what are the circumstances?

Brianna's Story: Lazy Students

Briana is a fourth grade teacher who is feeling frustrated while her class is talking. Let's dive into what she had to say to figure out why:

"My students are so lazy! They do various things when I teach, such as talking to each other rather than listening. They also get out of their desks or fidget when it's time to do independent work. They are so unmotivated. They don't care that they aren't learning. Why don't they care how much I do for them? They make me so frustrated."

Generally, the stories we tell ourselves have many more thoughts than circumstances. That's because the facts are pretty straightforward. The story behind it is where it gets a lot more interesting. Let's break it down into the thoughts and circumstances in Brianna's story:

Circumstances: Kids talk, fidget, and leave their desks during independent work time.

Thoughts: They are so lazy; They are unmotivated; They don't care about how much I do; They don't care if they are learning.

The exact behavior the kids have at the moment is not optional. Other people's actions are always a circumstance because we don't control them. We can have classroom management plans and do things on our side, but at this very moment, we can't force kids to take specific actions.

But Brianna's thought that "they are lazy" frustrates her. Let's pretend I'm coaching Brianna and ask her, "When you're frustrated, what do you do? And what do you **not** do that you might do if you weren't feeling so frustrated?"

Brianna says, "I don't know. I just can't stop thinking about how lazy they are. I go to my teacher besties to vent. I keep trying the same things, and they just aren't working. Sometimes, I get short with the kids or raise my voice or I need to sit back at my desk and take a breather because I can't take it anymore. Now that I think about it, I don't think I thought of trying anything new or asking the kids about why they keep doing this. I just send them to the principal's office when I get tired of their behavior. And then they return from his office with a lollipop! Every time. It does nothing."

Ironically, when Brianna thinks they are lazy, she gets frustrated. What does she do when she's frustrated? She doesn't try anything new and instead keeps trying the same things, like complaining to her friends and ruminating about how lazy the kids are. Brianna doesn't talk to the kids about it; instead, she sends them out of the room, raises her voice, and sits back at her desk. Even though she noticed that they come back with a lollipop each time they go to the principal's office, she keeps sending them to him without communicating about how this is reinforcing the behavior

Do you see the irony here? Brianna is saying her students are lazy, but one could argue that she is "lazy" with her teaching practices while trying the same thing repeatedly and expecting different results.

Now, there is nothing wrong with Brianna. I wouldn't want to call her a "lazy" teacher in any other setting. She's an incredible teacher who is in a thought loop about her students. But when using the model, we look at a single moment. We aren't looking at Brianna (as we use the model) as a whole person. We are not using the model to beat ourselves up. We are only looking at the results of what is happening when we think a particular thought, feel a certain way, and take specific actions to give ourselves awareness. And the "result" line of the model can change as soon as our "thought" changes.

Here is what Brianna's model for this thought might look like:

Circumstance: The kids are talking, fidgeting, and leaving their desks.
Thought: These kids are lazy.
Feeling: Frustrated.
Actions: I continue to spin in negative thoughts about my students, I complain to other teachers about it. I try the same things that weren't working again and again, instead of coming up with new solutions. I send kids to the principal's office. I do not have an open conversation with kids. I raise my voice and am short with kids. I check out by sitting at desk to take a breather
Result: I am currently being lazy in my classroom management practices.

We can see that this model isn't getting the results that Briana would desire. Her model would look a lot different if she were thinking, *"These are kids being kids,"* which may lead to indifference; or *"It's time to pivot,"* which might lead to curiosity or determination. You'll also notice that when she thinks "these kids are lazy," one of her actions is to continue to spin in negative thoughts. "Thinking" can be in the action line of the model, because we can go into thought spirals triggered by an initial thought. However, we only put one thought in the "thought" line of the model, as are looking at what is triggered by the initial thought.

Isn't it fascinating to see the results of a single thought? What if she'd thought something different? Instead of thinking her kids were lazy, what if she'd herself asked questions, such as "Why do I think they are acting this way right now?" or "What is something I haven't tried that I could try yet?" When we ask ourselves better questions, we get better answers! But her frustration was causing her to do different things, getting in the way of asking these potentially more helpful questions.

Her thoughts and feelings matter because she's not getting the result she wants. There's not anything inherently wrong with this situation or with Brianna. Many educators have probably felt similar to how Brianna did in this scenario. However, if I were to coach Brianna in this fictional story, she might realize what was happening and think, *"Wow! I had no clue this was happening!"* Often, in a coaching session, the client's face will soften, and their shoulders will relax from the awareness before we even move on to what could be more helpful. Once we know what we are doing is caused by what we are thinking and that we have the control, it can be a relief. Sometimes, awareness is all it takes.

At the same time, we don't want to be too swift to attempt to change our thoughts. Sitting in awareness to realize why we were thinking these thoughts in the first place is essential. Later, we'll create more intentional thoughts and pick new believable ones. But first, we need a profound understanding of the model. Let's dive into another example.

Maria's Story: The Big Audition

Maria is a homeschool mom who wants to audition for an orchestra. Let's take a look at her story:

"I haven't been a whole person or focusing on my hobbies. I've focused solely on my kids and their schooling, and I've been too busy to have time for anything else. But I decided it was time to do it anyway. I used to be an outstanding violinist before I had kids. I'm trying out for a local orchestra for a musical next week, but I'm not so good at playing anymore because it's been ten years since I've performed. I'm nervous I will be bad at it and bomb my audition. I'm not ready."

What are the thoughts, and what are the circumstances in Maria's story? Let's break it down now:

Circumstances: She has kids and has been homeschooling them. She plans to audition for a local orchestra for the first time in 10 years.

Thoughts: I've been too busy to do anything else; I used to be a good violinist, but I'm not a good violinist anymore; I'm going to be bad at it; I may bomb my audition; I haven't been a whole person, I haven't been focusing on my hobbies.

A lot of these are clear thoughts. *"I used to be a good violinist"* and *"I'm not a good violinist anymore"* are two sides of the same coin. A "good violinist" is up to interpretation. Someone may think Maria is an incredible violinist right now. They can't imagine picking up a bow and playing a chord.

Another might look at Maria and think, "She's no Lindsey Sterling!" Another person might not like Lindsey Sterling's take and think even she's a lousy violinist if they prefer more symphony-style violin music.

While those thoughts were more straightforward, some other statements from Maria in the story that I put in the "thought" category above might have surprised you. Many folks learning this work might think that being busy or not focusing on their hobbies would go in the "circumstance" line. But as we discussed in Chapter One, *"busy"* is always a thought (and one many teachers, homeschool parents, administrators, and people in general tend to have quite often). We know this because we could ask, "What does it mean to be busy?"

It's all up to interpretation. For Maria, she says she hasn't been focused on her hobbies at all because she's been homeschooling her kids. That is a thought that she's telling herself.

Now that we've clarified her original story's thoughts and circumstances, let's pretend I'm coaching Maria. She says, "I am just not ready for this audition. I'm feeling so nervous."

"It's understandable that you're feeling nervous, especially when you think you're not ready. When you're feeling nervous about this, what do you do?"

"Honestly? I overanalyze it. I'm hard on myself, and then my hands get shaky, so I don't play as well as when I'm having fun. Sometimes, I don't practice and try to find other things to do to get my mind off it. I also haven't told anyone about this audition because I don't want them to know if I fail. I keep thinking about how this audition could go wrong," Maria replies.

Through coaching, we might come to a model that looks something like this:

> **Circumstance:** Auditioning for local production.
> **Thought:** I'm not ready.
> **Feeling:** Nervous.
> **Actions:** I overanalyze when practicing. My hands get shaky. I don't play as well as when I am having fun. I find other things to do to get my mind off it instead of practicing. I say, "I'll do it later" and skip practicing. I don't tell people that I'm about to do this audition in case I "fail." I ruminate about the audition potentially going wrong. I compare myself to Lindsey Sterling.
> **Result:** I am ensuring that I'm not ready for the audition.

We can see clearly from Maria's actions that what she is doing (and not doing) is preventing her from being ready for her audition: precisely what she is worried about. As you understand the model, you'll find how much our initial thought ties into the results we see in our lives. As you reflect on this story, consider if there's been a time when you've recently seen this same pattern reflected in your own life.

As you read the final story, I want you to consider how you have stories similar to the ones that you have been reading going on in your mind. Maria's story is universal, showing that this work doesn't only apply to educators.

Kai's Story: Missed the Gym

Kai is a school counselor who is struggling with his after-school gym routine. Let's see what he has to say:

"I just signed up for Planet Fitness. My plan was to get there by 4:30 yesterday and stay and work out for at least half an hour. But then there was too much to do at work. It was a long day. I didn't leave my office until 5:00 after getting in at 7:00, so I didn't have time."

Now, let's pretend I'm coaching Kai. I ask him, "How do you feel when you think you have too much to do?"

"I'm just so upset. There's so much to do at school, and then I must go home and make dinner for me and my partner. The whole time I was making dinner, I kept thinking about how I didn't work out and was unsure if I was cut out for this. It's too much to do. I can't do it all," he says.

In this exchange, what are some of the circumstances and thoughts in Kai's story?

Circumstances: Kai signed up for Planet Fitness and planned to be there by 4:30. He left his office at 5:00 yesterday, missing his planned gym time.

Thoughts: I can't work out; There's too much to do at school; It was a long day; I'm upset at myself for not doing it; I'm such a mess, I can't do it all.

As we continue to talk about what was going on for him, we might go through a model together that looks something like this:

Circumstance: Got gym membership, planned to go at 4:30 after school yesterday.
Thought: I can't do it all.
Feeling: Inadequate.
Actions: I stay at school later. I don't go to the gym. I go right home and make dinner. I think about how I didn't work out. I question if I can do it. I'm not figuring out if there is another time I could work out. I'm not analyzing what could be done differently the next day. I'm calling myself a mess. I'm not giving myself grace.
Results: I am allowing myself not to do anything I want

Kai would realize he wasn't prioritizing himself by telling himself he had too much to do. While he has a job he wants to complete and a partner he wants to support, he neglects his own needs and desires. He also doesn't give himself any grace for missing one day at the gym. Missing the gym once meant he wasn't cut out for it, a prime example of all-or-nothing thinking.

Are there times you do the same thing? Do you ever make one mistake and make it mean that you are inadequate? The self-coaching model helps us realize when we do this instead of subconsciously ruminating in our thoughts.

The Self-Coaching Model Works... It's Backed by Research!

As you can see through these stories, the self-coaching model is a powerful tool that empowers individuals to cultivate self-awareness, driving personal growth. By examining our thoughts and beliefs, we gain clarity on the changes we want to make, fostering a sense of self-empowerment. This model offers flexibility, allowing us to engage in self-coaching sessions anytime and anywhere, without relying on scheduled appointments with a coach or therapist.

Developing these skills enables us to sustain a lifelong practice of self-awareness, reflection, and improvement. Through the self-coaching model, individuals can navigate challenges, overcome obstacles, and continue evolving on their personal development journey.

Studies have proven the effectiveness of the Self-Coaching Model. When I attended our recent life coaching mastermind, life coach and M.D. Sunny Smith was one of our presenters. She shared that several recent studies have proven the effectiveness of life coaching using our self-coaching model (Smith, 2023).

Her company, Empowered Women Physicians, did some research by compiling a large effect size to see the results of an eight-week coaching program for physicians. The results showed dramatic improvements in relieving burnout, improving professional fulfillment, increasing self-compassion, and building resilience.

Another 2020 study titled "Coaching for Primary Care Physician Well-being: A Randomized Trial and Follow-up Analysis" explores the impact of a six-session positive psychology-based coaching intervention on the well-being of Primary Care Physicians (PCPs) in the U.S. Facing burnout and declining well-being, 59 PCPs were randomly assigned to either receive coaching or be placed on a waitlist. The results revealed that those who enrolled in the life coaching experienced significantly decreased burnout and increased work engagement, psychological capacity, and job satisfaction compared to the waitlisted group. These positive effects were sustained over a six-month follow-up period. The findings suggest that coaching is a valuable and effective intervention for working professionals, relieving burnout and enhancing overall well-being (McGonagle et. al, 2020).

In our own practice, we've seen heartwarming stories. Janessa was one of our first clients, and on a recent call, she asked to come on and share an update with everyone: she received the all-clear for a year from her battle with cancer. Janessa discovered coaching after losing her father and contemplating leaving her teaching job due to burnout. Learning our coaching model prompted her to reevaluate her priorities and prioritize self-care. Shortly thereafter, she was diagnosed with breast cancer. Janessa credits her focus on self-care for catching the tumor early. She firmly believes in the power of coaching, as it helped her rearrange her life, leading to the joyous news of her cancer-free status!

Seeing educators, like Janessa, undergo remarkable transformations through the self-coaching model is truly inspiring. It's a reminder that these changes are within reach for anyone willing to prioritize this approach. Remember, it's not just about consuming information—it's about taking action. Just as you can't lift weights once and expect to stay fit, consistent effort is key here too. Think of it like classroom management; it's an ongoing process, not a one-time discussion. That's why I refer to thought work as "mind management," it's a daily practice that simplifies everything else in life.

There are several ways to do this. One option is to work with a certified life coach or therapist to help you with this work (the Educate & Rejuvenate Club is a fantastic option for coaching). Having a mentor to help you see your blind spots can help make the transformations happen even faster.

To see an example of life coaching in action, be sure to check out the videos linked in your Educate & Rejuvenate workbook (www.teachergoals.com/educate-resources). From these clips, you'll see how powerful it is to have a coach by your side. But whether or not you decide to work with a coach personally, you can learn so much simply from observing these sessions and reflecting on the included questions, as well as listening to the FREE Educate & Rejuvenate podcast.

How to Utilize Self-Coaching

While a trained coach can help you notice any blind spots, you can also do a lot of work through self-coaching. All you need is a pen, paper, your brain, and as little as 10 minutes daily to see a drastic shift in your mindset. You have all the tools and knowledge to do this simply by getting this far in the book. You can do this!

There is a simple three-step process that you can use to self-coach:

1) Get a pen and paper and do a "thought download" to get everything inside your head down on paper. It's like you're downloading what's in your brain, so it no longer has to stay stuck there. You can do a general thought download and let anything that comes to your head flow from pen to paper, or do one for a specific area of your life (teaching, parenting, etc.).

As you write, don't judge yourself or filter anything; remember, it's for your eyes only! We also don't want to consider whether every statement we write would fall under "circumstances" or "thoughts" just yet. The point is to get whatever comes to your mind down on paper. Even if you only follow this step of the process, it will help clear your headspace, and you'll likely breathe a sigh of relief as you let it all go.

2) Read through your thought download like an outside observer. Think of it as if you are reading one of the "stories" from Brianna, Maria, and Kai earlier in this chapter. List all the "circumstances" and "thoughts" in your thought download. If you need more help being objective, feel free to have a trusted friend read it over. Or feel free to head over to Educate & Rejuvenate Club; my team and I will also be happy to support you!

3) Finally, pick one thought from your thought download that you want to focus on and start a Model. Write the letters

"C," "T," "F," "A," and "R" vertically down the page (these letters stand for "Circumstance," "Thought," "Feeling," "Action," and "Result"). Then ask yourself, what is the circumstance you are thinking that thought about? How does it make you feel? What do you do when you feel this way? What *don't* you do when you think this way? And what is the result of those actions and inactions?

C _____

T _____

F _____

A _____

R _____

As you embark on your self-coaching journey, remember that you possess all the tools and knowledge necessary to effect meaningful change in your life. Armed with just a pen, paper, and a mere 10 minutes, you have the power to transform your mindset and outlook. As you self-coach, you may notice feelings arise as part of the process.

4

Understanding Our Feelings

As we've learned with the self-coaching model, our thoughts are the catalyst that shapes our lives. But our thoughts are not the only part of the model we want to consider. Where do we fully experience life? In our feelings. **Everything we want in our lives is because of how we think it will make us feel.**

We not only want to examine how thoughts inside our heads impact our emotions, we also want to observe what is happening inside our bodies and bring attention to that in our minds. When we observe what's happening in our bodies, we look at feelings, sensations, and whether or not we are regulated. The tools we use to monitor what is going on in our bodies are called somatic tools.

In the modern day, many of us have learned to disconnect from our bodies and let our heads take control. Because of this, the top-down approach of thought work feels closer to what we are used to. Getting in touch with our bodies can feel very foreign, so these tools may take more time and practice to master. If this happens to you, don't worry—it is a normal part of the process.

If you ever try to work with your thoughts and feel resistance, take a breath. You likely need to connect with what your body is telling you.

We Try to Do Anything but Feel Our Feelings

We think we feel our feelings, but frequently, we do everything we can to avoid leaning into our emotions. But the effort is futile. A quote widely attributed to Austrian neurologist Sigmund Freud says, "Unexpressed emotions will never die. They are buried alive and will come forth later in uglier ways (Vahrmeyer, 2021)." In other words, we can try to bury our feelings, but they're still there, and like zombies, they'll arise and wreak havoc if they aren't dealt with. That's why it's so important to allow and process our feelings.

The problem is, most of us don't do that. Since we don't want to feel pain, we try to do anything but feel it. In my life coaching certification, my mentor, Brooke Castillo, taught me the four strategies we subconsciously use to deal with our emotions: resist, react, avoid, and allow. Each of these strategies has the same goal: we want to feel better, and these things will provide relief.

However, when we resist, react, or avoid, the relief is temporary because it prevents us from becoming an observer and blocks the release of the emotion. Only allowing our feelings will ultimately enable us to feel better, but without conscious effort, this is not what we usually do.

As you read through the following stories and descriptions of the four strategies we utilize with our emotions, ask yourself which ones you do most often.

Resisting

Mr. Rodriguez, a charter school administrator, grappled with impending decisions as dwindling enrollment, budget cuts, and staff restructuring loomed. He knew his choices would deeply impact his beloved teachers and staff.

Despite the weight of these decisions, Mr. Rodriguez maintained a stoic facade, as vulnerability was frowned upon in the administrative culture. He bore the emotional burden alone, unwilling to share his fears with colleagues or family. Yet, his emotions showed in the lines on his face and weariness in his eyes. It was evident he was at his wit's end when he started having panic attacks.

Mr. Rodriguez isn't alone in this struggle—it's a common theme among educators. In the demanding world of teaching, there's this unspoken rule that we must always remain composed and strong, no matter what. Expressing vulnerability is often seen as a weakness, so we find ourselves burying our emotions, both at work and at home. We're trapped in this cycle where we're expected to show resilience, even when it's taking a toll on our well-being

But we can't keep this up forever. Resisting our emotions might seem like the right thing to do in the short term, but in the long run, it's harmful to our mental and emotional health. When we resist our emotions, it's like trying to hold a door shut, only adding pressure. This "bottling up" of feelings might delay the inevitable, but eventually, we will find ourselves reacting to these.

Reacting

Samantha, a devoted fifth-grade teacher, struggled with balancing her teaching duties and caring for her aging parents. Despite her efforts to put on a "happy face," the stress weighed heavily on her. When confronted with an angry parent's call and news of her father's declining health on the same day, Samantha felt overwhelmed. In a moment of impulsivity, she resigned mid-year, shocking her principal and colleagues.

Upon reflection, she realized her decision stemmed from a desire to regain control over her chaotic life rather than a genuine desire to leave teaching and her students. Samantha's situation was a classic overreaction. Instead of feeling and processing her emotions, she let them take the lead and resigned without fully thinking it through. Reacting to our emotions can manifest in an emotional outburst, such as Samantha's quick resignation.

I had my own experience earlier this year with an exchange with my husband regarding our homeschooling. We tag-team our homeschooling since we both work on our own companies from home. During a busy season at my company, I let him take the reins. When I returned to my homeschooling days, the kids weren't as far in their curriculum as I'd expected. And that's when "mama bear" came out.

I stormed up the stairs as the gravity of the situation hit me. He couldn't be trusted to teach our kids. I'd have to do it all.

"I'm taking over the homeschooling!" I declared as I stormed into our homeschool room. "The kids are behind, so this isn't working. I'm going to hire a tutor to help me." Stunned by the abrupt outburst, my husband froze. The pain on his face showed me how much I'd overreacted.

My heart sank. "I'm sorry," I sighed. I realized I'd let the emotions get to me. When we had a rational conversation about the situation, I realized that he was doing more than it looked like on the page, he just wasn't teaching only "by the book," something I value as well!

Chances are you can probably think of a time you reacted to your emotions, whether an emotional outburst or making rash decisions based on your feelings without checking in with yourself.

For example, if you're worrying about not having enough money, you might make financial decisions out of scarcity, making abrupt budget cuts that impact your overall well-being, such as stopping therapy or continuing education. If you took some time to observe your thoughts and get out of fear, you might make a different decision. We know we are reacting because we are clearly acting out of emotion rather than with our rational mind. In the process, we aren't moving through the emotion.

Avoiding

Arum, in her first year as an instructional coach, felt the weight of her responsibilities after another exhausting 10-hour day. Despite her dedication, things weren't going as smoothly as she hoped. She faced resistance from other teachers, leaving her overwhelmed and doubting herself. As problems lingered, she grappled with feelings of anxiety and inadequacy. Her heart rate increased as she worried about what everyone else was thinking about her. Unwilling to confront these emotions, she instinctively disengaged mentally, seeking to avoid them at any cost.

She headed to the pantry to grab a bag of chips, got out her phone, and scrolled while chowing down. She saw a silly cat video that made her laugh, and then tagged her friend in the latest teacher meme. Then, she saw a Facebook ad for a new pair of shoes and instantly clicked the "buy it now" button, giving her another dopamine hit. That would make her feel better and make the anxiety go away, right?

Does this sound familiar to you at all? Many of us do these types of things when we try to avoid our emotions, and that's precisely what Arum was doing as she mindlessly ate chips while spending hours doom-scrolling. Avoiding emotions is when we do anything to avoid feeling the emotion. This can include overeating, overdrinking, shopping, overworking, etc.

In the life coaching industry, we often call this "buffering" because it resembles the rainbow-colored cursor that pops up when Apple devices get stuck. This spinning wheel is frequently given the melodramatic name of the "spinning wheel of death." Usually, this means that the computer is frozen and will be stuck "buffering" until you do something about it. The spinning wheel will not disappear until we restart the computer.

When we are buffering, we are doing the same thing. We may be moving forward and doing something, but our actions keep us stuck on a hamster wheel. The only way out is to allow and process our emotions.

Allowing

What if instead of resisting, reacting, or avoiding their emotions, the educators in the previous stories had taken a moment to allow and process their feelings instead?

Mr. Rodriguez, the school principal resisting the emotions he felt due to his administrative decisions, might finally feel the relief of the mounting pressure release. Only by allowing himself to process his emotions could he bridge the gap between leadership and empathy and make the best decisions for all parties involved, ensuring resilience amid the challenges ahead.

Samantha, the fifth-grade teacher who sent in a hasty resignation, may have taken a moment to center herself and realized she didn't want to quit before it was too late. She would still have the job she loved but may have found support to help with the overwhelm. All the while, she might have realized that she needed to give herself grace and self-compassion, knowing she was doing her best.

Finally, the new instructional coach, Arum, might have felt her feelings of inadequacy and overwhelm simmer down rather than spending hours scrolling on social media. Instead, she may have been able to use the time for some true rejuvenation, such as a meaningful call with a friend or journaling to get her thoughts down. She may also have one less pair of cute but unnecessary shoes in her closet (and the money in her bank account).

This is the magic that happens when we allow and process our emotions by noting the sensations in our body and allowing the sensations to move through us. When we process them, the feelings become less overbearing. Allowing our emotions without judgment is an essential part of being an observer of ourselves.

How To Allow Our Emotions

Below, I have outlined strategies you can use to move through and process your feelings. Allowing our feelings may be crucial, but the question remains: How do we do it? There's no magic formula, but the good news is that there are strategies that will help you on your journey. You can utilize any of the tools below, in any order, to help you move through your feelings.

Naming Our Emotions

Our goal with allowing our emotions is to observe our feelings, and naming our emotions is one of the best ways do this. It's incredible how something as simple as naming our emotions can help us alleviate the feeling, but it works. It's not just a trick; putting our feelings into words (also called affect labeling) has been proven to help people navigate through solid emotions.

In a 2007 Psychology study from University of California, Los Angeles (UCLA), the researchers used a brain imaging technique to understand what happens when people name their feelings.

The findings suggested that labeling their emotions reduced the response of a brain region called the amygdala. The amygdala is associated with processing negative emotions, meaning that we are likely to feel emotions such as stress or fear when it is involved. Additionally, there was increased activity in another brain region called the right ventrolateral prefrontal cortex (RVLPFC), which plays a role in regulating emotions, when the subjects participated in affect labeling. As the activity of the amygdala decreased, the activity of the RVPLC increased (Lieberman et. al, 2007).

Naming the feelings sends calming neurotransmitters to the amygdala, aiding study participants in regulating their emotions while calming their minds and bodies. Dr. Dan Siegel coined the term "Name it to Tame It" as a simple way to remember this process: when we name the emotions, they simmer down (Siegel & Bryson, 2011).

In an interview with Dr. Brene Brown for her book *Atlas of the Heart*, Dr. Susan David said, "Learning to label our emotions with more nuanced vocabulary can be absolutely transformative." David points out that without an adequate emotional vocabulary, expressing our needs becomes challenging, hindering our ability to receive the necessary support from others (Brown, 2021). And, as we learned from the 2007 UCLA psychology study, the act of affect labeling is linked to improved emotional regulation and psychological well-being.

As you're naming your emotions, pay attention to the subtleties of your experience, as this will give you a greater depth of understanding as you become an observer. For example:

If you feel like things are too much when you look at your

to-do list for your lesson planning the next week, are you stressed (too much to do, but you're handling it), or are you overwhelmed (the load is higher and you cannot handle it)?

If you find yourself thinking something wrong about yourself while you're teaching, are you feeling guilt (which stems from thinking along the lines of "I did something bad"), or are you feeling shame (which stems from thinking something like, "I am bad")?

There's no right or wrong to the bullet points above. These just help you realize the nuance of different emotions to help you label your experience as authentically as possible. At the same time, don't overthink labeling your feelings, either. I have had clients on a coaching call who struggle to decide their emotions. Maybe it's this, or perhaps it's that. When this happens, I usually explain that defining our feelings is as much an art as a science. Over time, you can work to strengthen your vocabulary, but don't let choosing the perfect word keep you from labeling your emotion and processing it.

Breathing

"Breathing in, I calm body and mind. Breathing out, I smile. Dwelling in the present moment, I know this is the only moment." This quote from Thích Nhất Hạnh (Vietnamese monk, peace activist, author, and teacher) summed up the power of our breath (Hanh, 1987). The practice of breath control has been a staple in Eastern cultures, and we are starting to appreciate the practice of connecting with our breath in Western culture, as well. Breathing with intention is one of the most powerful ways to calm our bodies, bring ourselves to the present moment, and ground ourselves as we process our emotions.

So how do we harness this breathing power? In "The

Breathing Cure," Patrick McKeown emphasizes the importance of slow, light, and deep breathing. Rapid, shallow breathing deprives us of its benefits. Sometimes, we even confuse a "deep" breath as a "big" breath, thinking that taking a deep breath is about the amount of air intake. However, quality over quantity is key, so avoid overfilling the lungs. To center ourselves, we can aim for six breaths per minute, focusing on gentle, deep breaths- meaning that the breath reaches the diaphragm. Just a minute of deliberate, mindful breathing can anchor us in the present and empower us to manage our emotions effectively.

When appropriately utilized, our breath can also calm our emotions, regulate our nervous system, reduce stress hormones, release tension, and more. Breathing mindfully is the ultimate opportunity for self-nurturing, and it's something we always have time for, no matter how busy we might think we are. Even if you are in a heated conversation with a coworker or are responding to a child's meltdown, you can take a few seconds to pause and take an intentional breath. It can make all the difference in how we handle our emotions.

Tapping into our breath allows us to calm our bodies. As Thích Nhất Hạnh says, "Feelings come and go like clouds in a windy sky, conscious breathing is my anchor (Nhất Hạnh 1997)." We can feel our emotions come and go when we connect to our breath.

Meditation

About six months ago, I felt overwhelmed with everything in my life. Between all the aspects of my business, homeschooling my kids, planning our winter event, and writing this book, the ruminating thoughts were taking over. I was observing my thoughts and realizing they were getting in the way, but I was out of touch with my body.

During a session, I shared my struggles with my life coach, and she encouraged me to "stop, drop, and meditate" whenever the overwhelm came up. I previously had a great habit of meditating, but I'd gotten out of the practice. As I started to make meditation a priority again, I could connect more with my body and move through the stress and emotion.

When we meditate, we are putting the rest of our lives on pause, allowing us to sit with our emotions. Meditation teacher, psychologist, and author Tara Brach explains in her book *Radical Acceptance* that a "pause is a suspension of activity, a time of temporary disengagement when we are no longer moving toward any goal.... The pause can occur amid almost any activity and can last for an instant, for hours, or seasons of our life.... We may pause in the midst of meditation to let go of thoughts and reawaken our attention to the breath.... You might try it now: Stop reading and sit there, doing "no thing," and simply notice what you are experiencing (Brach, 2000)."

While meditation helped me to relax, move through my emotions, and refocus, it isn't just for self-care. In fact, it actually changes our biology! Joe Dispenza shares that his team of researchers took brain scans of participants in their meditation workshops using quantitative electroencephalogram measurements. The difference was dramatic. The participants' brains functioned more synchronized and coherently after just a few days at a meditation retreat. Their studies also showed changes in heart rate variability, showing external data to reflect the internal changes from within. He says, "We know that it takes a clear intention (a coherent brain) and an elevated emotion (a coherent heart) to begin to change a person's biology from living in the past to living in the future. The mind and body—thoughts and feelings—also seem to influence the matter. And that's how you create reality (Dispenza, 2017)."

Are you ready to start processing your emotions by

meditating? As you meditate, you will shift your brain biology so you can more easily allow your feelings as they come your way. There are two types of meditation:

Guided meditation: As the name suggests, this type of meditation is when you have a video, audio, or live instructor as your guide. If you're new to the practice, I recommend guided meditation. It is much easier to stick to it when a guide tells you exactly what to do, which can also help you keep your mind from wandering. You can find some recommended apps in the resources section in the back of this book.

Self Meditation: This is where your meditation is self-guided. There is no audio or video to follow. Once you feel comfortable with guided meditation, you can try it. You will deepen your practice and get even more in tune with yourself. Getting to the point where you can use self-meditation shows you have reached the next level in your meditation practice, when you can calm your mind and body purely based on your intentions.

Process Emotions Through a Guided Practice

You may not be sure how to get started with these strategies. Try this guided practice below where you can name emotions, breathe, and meditate. Follow along as you read these pages, or download an audio of this practice along with your **Educate & Rejuvenate workbook and resources**:

- Start by taking three slow, light, and deep breaths.
- Notice the feeling that is there without judgment.
- *What is this feeling called?*
- *What does it feel like in my body?*

- Do a body scan and notice where it feels from the top of your head to the tip of your toes.
- *If it were a color, what color would it be?*
- *Is it hard or soft?*
- *Is it open or closed?*
- Remind yourself- I am feeling (name the emotion).
- Breathe it in.
- While in mindful meditation, stay present for a few minutes before opening your eyes.

Figure 4.1
Guided Practice

You Can Navigate Your Emotions

My mentor Brooke Castillo's statement blew my mind: "The worst thing that can happen to us is a negative emotion (Castillo, 2015)." This statement initially shocked me because I thought that much worse things could happen. Just look at the news or lose and grieve a loved one, and somebody will convince you that this statement is nonsense. You might think the worst thing that could happen isn't an emotion, but losing a loved one, or racism, sexism, cancer, or any of the other terrible things in this world.

Consider this: you feel those emotions because you care. They reflect what's important to you, an inevitable part of being human. It's not about denying these feelings; it's acknowledging that they're a natural part of life. We experience negative emotions about 50% of the time and positive ones the rest. This awareness reminds us of our resilience—we're built to navigate these emotions.

Emotions are simply sensations in our bodies. Emotion alone isn't able to harm us. We can ride the waves of our emotions by utilizing the strategies outlined in this chapter. This chapter's simple yet powerful strategies allow you to move through your emotions. As you allow an emotion, you will notice it simmer down and become less overbearing.

You may also find that, at times, some of these tools may work better than others. For example, right after my postpartum anxiety attack, breathing exercises were not ideal for me. Because I had experiences with losing my breath and being jolted awake, whenever I was asked to do breathing exercises by my therapist or life coach, it would trigger a stress response.

As we journey through the intricacies of understanding and controlling our emotions, it's essential to understand that there isn't only one right way to ride the waves. The important thing is for you to trust yourself to pick the strategy you need at the moment by listening to your body. Your body is your compass. Empowerment starts with the conscious choice to tune in and use its wisdom as you navigate your emotional landscape.

5

Befriending Our Nervous System

Picture this. It's a chilly October day, and Jessica (also known as "Miss Smith" by her kindergarten class) is ready to take on the world. She has her Starbucks pumpkin spice latte in hand as she walks into the school building, waves to her co-teachers, and starts getting herself situated for the day ahead.

As she finishes her prep, the bell rings. She greets each child with a "high-five" as they walk through her door. Hearing their sweet giggles and "hellos" always makes her morning.

Of course, it isn't all sunshine and rainbows. These are five and six-year-olds we're talking about, after all. While Jessica typically keeps her cool with the occasional skinned knee or an argument over a glue stick, today throws her a curveball. Ms. La Rue, her principal, walks in for a surprise observation while the kids come in from recess (cue her heart in her throat)

Suddenly, Jessica's pulse rushes, and her stomach feels a lurch. Her breath becomes shallow and short, and she feels a heat wave of nervousness as her body responds to this unexpected visit. Even though she was well prepared for the day, her brain goes blank.

Dazed, she tells her students to head to their chairs as she tries to collect her thoughts. Instead, she nervously shuffles through her lesson plan pages, but the words on the page don't seem to register in her mind. Fumbling through the lesson, she's in a consistent state of brain fog and lacks the clarity she usually has when teaching.

There is a rational explanation for why this highly effective, well-prepared teacher could freeze when her principal walks into the room. Jessica's nervous system is doing its job to keep her safe and identify potential dangers.

Even though she has a great working relationship with her principal (who was simply doing her job by coming in to do the observation), something made Jessica feel "unsafe." Her nervous system was signaling alarm bells and she experienced a "freeze" stress response, which is a physiological response that she had no control over.

Chances are, you can relate to the "freeze" response described above, whether you experienced it during a teacher observation, a job interview, or a difficult conversation. And that is because your nervous system is doing its job.

What is the Nervous System?

Most of us understand that we have a nervous system, but we may not know much beyond that. Some teachers may have even touched on it or mentioned it in human body studies that we have taught. However, we may not be able to describe what it does, since its functions are automatic and happen behind the scenes. We don't realize how it is at work in our everyday lives.

Essentially, our nervous system allows our brain and body to communicate. But if you're like me and like to know the nitty-gritty, geeky details, I've got you covered.

The nervous system is divided into two primary parts: the central nervous system (the brain and spinal cord) and the peripheral nervous system (the other nerves throughout our bodies). While the central nervous system is responsible for processing information and sending instructions to and from the peripheral nervous system, the peripheral nervous system's role is to transmit sensory input to the central nervous system and carry out motor commands from the central nervous system (Vallie & Juber, 2022).

From there, the peripheral nervous system divides into two sub-systems: the somatic nervous system and the autonomic nervous system. The somatic nervous system is in charge of voluntary movement (such as raising your hand or walking) and relaying information from the senses of sound, smell, taste, and touch to the brain (your sense of sight connects directly to the brain via the retina and optic nerve).

The autonomic nervous system is in charge of everything our bodies do that is out of our control. However, that's not all: we have two more sub-systems! The autonomic nervous system includes the parasympathetic system and the sympathetic system.

The parasympathetic nervous system keeps our bodies functioning during everyday situations, when we are in a regulated state. It's why we don't have to think about breathing, digesting our food, and keeping our heart rate regular. Imagine if we had to think about doing all of these things. We would never have time for anything else!

On the other hand, the sympathetic nervous system is in charge of looking after our survival. Its ultimate goal is our safety. Like a smoke detector, it is constantly scanning to check if we are safe or in danger, and it takes over when we are in what it identifies as dangerous situations.

Whenever a threat is perceived, the sympathetic nervous system sends a signal to the amygdala, the part of your brain that tells your body to release cortisol and adrenaline in response to stress. When our nervous system is activated, we go into one of four stress responses: fight, flight, freeze, or fawn.

Stress Responses

These four stress responses have been essential for the survival of humans. For example, if we were to be attacked by a bear, we wouldn't be able to think our way through what to do fast enough, and that's why these survival instincts kick into gear. Our body automatically goes into action mode, turning up the sensations needed to get through the threat and turning down the less necessary functions until the danger has passed and we are safe (Catillo, 2022).

Here's what that looks like for each stress response (and when and why we go into each one):

Fight: Our body has assessed the threat and believes it can overcome and fight against it. For example, if a bear attacks us and our body thinks we can fight back, the body automatically responds by preparing for the physical demands of fighting back against the bear, such as increased adrenaline production and heightened alertness.

Flight: When our belief in overcoming the threat is low, but we can escape, our body will initiate a flight response. We cannot fight the bear, so we run away. This reaction fuels the body with a surge of adrenaline, aiding us in rapidly running away from the threat of the bear faster than we could in ordinary circumstances.

Freeze: The freeze response occurs when our body identifies the threat but assesses that neither fighting nor fleeing the danger is viable. Instead, the body conserves energy, and nonessential functions (such as the immune and digestive systems) slow down. You may have noticed yourself getting sick more when you are stressed, because *stress can* make you sick! In the case of a bear attack, this could include lying motionless, hoping not to attract attention or escalate the situation.

Fawn: The fawn response happens when all other reactions—fight, flight, or freeze—feel futile. Instead, we try to appease the threat by showing submission. Rather than trying to fight or escape the danger, we are trying to please the threat. During a bear attack, this may involve gestures like speaking in a soft voice or backing up slowly to communicate non-aggressiveness.

These responses occur on a spectrum and aren't always exclusive. We might transition from one response to another during any given encounter based on the evolving perception of the threat.

These actions happen automatically. For example, let's say our house is on fire and we must get away. We don't have a lot of time to think about all of our options. Our bodies will respond automatically, perhaps going into a "fight" response to grab a fire extinguisher, or going into a "flight" stress response when we realize the fire is too big to put out. It will give us the extra adrenaline to get ourselves (and our families) out quicker than we could without these stress responses. We can thank our sympathetic nervous system for doing whatever we can to survive any threat that comes our way and get ourselves back to safety.

However, with every benefit comes its drawbacks. The flip side of this benefit is that our sympathetic nervous system is similar to a smoke detector; it can't tell the difference between when it goes off because of a five-alarm fire in our house or simply because you burned toast. You are physically in danger in one situation, but not in the other. Your sympathetic nervous system will signal the alarm either way.

Today, we may not be regularly affected by stressors such as bear attacks or house fires, but the stress responses still impact us daily. That's because the same instincts that help us survive threats that bring us physical danger can also trigger stress responses simply from our everyday challenges, such as when Jessica's principal walked in the room for a surprise observation.

Here are some more scenarios in which we might see how each of the four stress responses look in everyday life:

- Jason is commuting to work when another driver suddenly cuts him off. Before thinking of what to do next, he experiences a "fight" response and immediately slams on his breaks, tenses up, and yells some choice words toward the other driver.
- When a clown with a chainsaw jumps out at 14-year-old Katarina in a haunted house, she has a "fight" response, jumps, and screams instantly, even though logically, she knows she is safe.
- During independent work, seven-year-old Diego tries to finish his math assignment but doesn't grasp the concepts. As his body identifies the threat of what may happen if he does not complete his assignment, he clenches his fists and yells, "I can't do this!" (fight), and then gets up and wanders the classroom (flight).
- Homeschool mom Rachel feels so overwhelmed by teaching her four kids and running her online business. When a text comes with a reminder that it's her turn to lead the homeschool co-op, she dreams of packing her bags and driving with no end in sight (flight). But when she realizes she can't, she shuts down and can't seem to start a single item on her to-do list (freeze).
- First-grade teacher Adrienne has concerns as she listens to a discussion about how a new policy will affect her work at a faculty meeting. Since no one else has expressed any concerns,

she doesn't feel she can do anything to change it. She goes along with it and stays engaged in the discussion at a surface level while neglecting to address her own needs (fawn).
- An unknown loud noise crashes down the hall, and the class erupts in terror. Both the teacher and the students immediately go into various stress responses. The teacher yells, then ensures that her students are okay (fight). Two of her students run toward the door (flight). Meanwhile, three of her students are not moving (freeze). Another student is silently praying (fawn).

As you can see, we often end up in one of these stress responses. It's a sign that our autonomic nervous system is working. However, getting stuck in a stress response can make life more difficult.

Even when the threat is gone, our bodies don't immediately get the memo that the danger is over. This happens whether this is a genuine threat to our safety *(we think we are about to be attacked by a bear, but then the bear runs away and we are no longer in danger)* or perceived danger *(Jessica has a surprise classroom observation, but it has ended, and her principal has left the room).*

We may still feel the heightened sensations of our stress response long after the threat has passed. Even though the stressor may be gone, we haven't dealt with the stress itself. They are two different things, and we need to treat them as such. The question is... what can we do to help our bodies know that we are safe to escape the stress response? We need to complete the stress response cycle.

Completing the Stress Response Cycle

When we are dysregulated, telling ourselves that "we're good" doesn't fix the problem. In the book *Burnout*, twin sisters Emily and Amelia Nagoski explain, "Completing the cycle isn't an intellectual decision; it's a physiological shift.... You give your body what it needs and allow it to do what it does...in the time it requires (Nagoski & Nagoski, 2020)."

Figure 5.1
How to Complete Stress Cycle

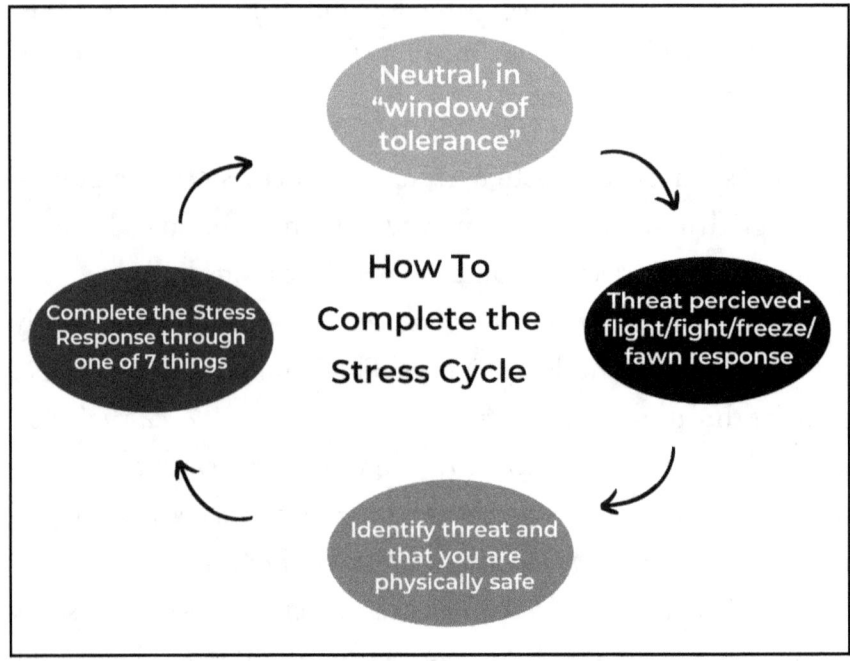

Emily & Amelia share the following seven ways to complete the stress response cycle:

Physical Activity is, by far, the most effective way to complete the stress cycle. When there is a threat, the first thing our body wants to do, if possible, is run away from it. Physical activity is the best way to tell your body that you survived the threat and are safe. Any movement will help: walking outside, doing yoga, swimming, or riding a bike. You can also simply turn on some your favorite music and dance your heart out while no one is watching.

I will do this with my kids and turn on silly songs they love, such as "It's Raining Tacos" or "What Does The Fox Say?" Do whatever is most enjoyable for you. Exercise is not only for your physical health, but also your mental and emotional health.

Breathing helps us move through our emotions and regulates the nervous system. As we learned from Peter McKewon in the last chapter, it is ideal for us to breathe "slowly, lightly, and deeply." Jeff Sorensen, founder of breathARMY, explains that when we breathe quickly and with greater volume, our nervous system becomes more activated. The heightened activation readies us for activity, leading to an increased heart rate and the release of chemicals like adrenaline in our system (Sorensen, n.d.)

Conversely, slowing down and softening our breath tends to induce relaxation. Notably, our exhalations play a significant role in calming the nervous system. We can relax our body by consciously extending and slowing down our exhalations. Our breath is like a remote control for our nervous system, directly impacting the signals our brain sends to the body and vice versa. We can regulate our bodies by bringing our attention to our breath.

Connecting with others around us in a friendly way signals to our bodies that we are safe. It can be anything from having a five minute conversation with a coworker during your prep period or calling a best friend. It can even be as simple as sparking a conversation with your cashier as you smile and ask them how their day is going, or complimenting the waitress by telling her that you love her shoes. Finding safe people to connect with is vital. Our bodies will know if they feel "safe" to us because we will feel relaxed around them rather than stressed. We crave human connection, so connecting with others around us signals to our bodies that it is okay to calm down now; good people surround us, and we are safe.

Affection can help us regulate our nervous system if verbal connection isn't enough. Touch is a powerful way to connect on a deeper level. A straightforward way to do this is with an eight-second hug each day, a concept I originally learned from following the late #SaveTheKids advocate, Collin Kartchner, on Instagram (Johnson, 2020). A hug of at least eight seconds can help us release oxycontin and increase our serotonin levels, helping our nervous system regulate (Peterson, 2023). A great acronym for this is **H.U.G.: H**old on tight **U**ntil you relax and **G**row your bond (Escalante, 2020).

These hugs can be from a partner, friend, or even ourselves if we don't have anyone around us when we need support. Remember Kristin Neff, the self-compassion author and researcher from Chapter One? She shares that an easy way to comfort ourselves is to hug ourselves. It might sound silly, but you can feel your body calm down from physical touch—even when it comes from ourselves!

Laughter is a natural medicine that aids in regulating the nervous system. The joyous act of laughter releases endorphins, reduces stress hormones, and promotes well-being, contributing to a balanced and healthy mind. So turn on your favorite comedy show. If you can do this while connecting with others or snuggling with a partner (getting connection, affection, and laughter all in one), it's even better!

Crying can also be a great way to release stress. We often feel a massive release when we let it all out with a 10-minute cry because it completes the stress response cycle. Similarly to how I suggested pulling out a comedy to laugh, you could pull out your favorite tear-jerker if you need help releasing your built-up emotions and regulating your body.

Creative Expression can help our bodies recover from stress, too! During one of the shows during her 2024 Eras Tour, Grammy-winning recording artist Taylor Swift opened up about the process of creating her next album, The Tortured Poets Department. She said, "This album...more than any of my albums, I *needed* to make it. It was a lifeline for me, just the things I was going through, the things I was writing about. It kind of reminded me why songwriting is something that gets me through my life. I've never had an album where I needed songwriting more than I needed it [now] (Yahoo! News, 2024)."

Just as songwriting helped Swift express her emotions, we can regulate ourselves through creative expressions. Big emotions are encouraged in the arts and can even improve our craft. We can express ourselves through writing, storytelling, painting, music, theater, and more. As educators, we can add creative activities to our teaching schedule to help students and ourselves complete the stress cycle regularly. These are some of the top ways to complete the cycle, but another way (not listed above) may work well for you, too. Listen to your body and give yourself what you need.

How do you know when you complete the stress cycle? According to Emily and Amelia Nagoski, it's like knowing you are full when you finish a meal (Nagoski & Nagoski, 2020). You can feel it, and you just know that even though it may take a minute, it may be easier or quicker for some people to identify than others. The key is to trust yourself so that you will be able to sense when you've moved into this state.

Another clue to show that you have completed the cycle is if you can use the rest of the tools in this book by observing your thoughts, emotions, and actions. You cannot access your rational thinking brain when you are in a stress response, so if you can quickly notice your thoughts or feelings, you have completed the cycle.

While we are human and will always experience the stress cycle, the key is to notice when we are in one and complete it sooner rather than being stuck inside the cycle. We can also build habits to help us regularly complete our stress cycles, such as scheduling exercise into our routine or a regular book club for the community

We can also work towards increasing what Dr. Dan Siegel called the "window of tolerance". Our window of tolerance is the amount of stress our system can take before it gets hyperaroused or hypoaroused (Wright & Sills, 2022). While we will never eradicate the stress cycle, our tolerance window increases as we increase our resilience. As we do this, we can see the time between our stress cycles increase, meaning we won't get dysregulated as often.

Trauma Is When We Get Stuck in a Dysregulated State

While trauma is not a recurring theme in this book, it is essential to consider how it may impact your experience as you dive into personal development and connect to your mind and body. Trauma can be a scary-sounding word, and it may not be something you'd want to consider that you have. And there is a chance you have also experienced it in some form. According to Peter Levine, PhD, "Psychological trauma can happen to anyone when they perceive a situation as a threat and are unable to complete a satisfactory fight, flight or freeze response (Levine & Curlander, 2022)." Note this would also include the fawn response we discussed.

Many people experience trauma because of experiences in their childhood because trauma makes a more lasting impression on the brain while it is still developing. Adverse childhood experiences include abuse (physical, emotional, or sexual), neglect (physical or emotional), and household dysfunction (mental illness, incarcerated parent, domestic violence, substance abuse, or divorce). According to the Centers for Disease Control and Prevention (CDC), over 63% of adults have at least one adverse childhood experience, and 17.3% reported experiencing four or more (2023). If you experienced any of these things, you might be even more prone to trauma. However, trauma can be experienced at any point in life when we get stuck in a stress response cycle.

Trauma is generally discussed in two categories. "Big T" trauma is what many of us tend to think of, typically a significant event in one's life or a life-threatening situation. Big T trauma includes abuse, school shootings, natural disasters, car accidents, combat, the death of a parent as a child, or any significant event that could cause trauma. "Small t" traumas are less severe or repeated events that, while they typically don't involve disaster, still exceed our ability to cope and prevent us from completing the stress response cycle, such as bullying or betrayal in relationships. These can be harder to identify since there may not be one inciting incident, and we may not consider that they could have created trauma (Barbash, 2023).

Educators may experience trauma on the job from experiences including the loss of a student, parental conflicts, or even violence. The long-term impacts of burnout could also result in not leaving the stress response cycle. Let's not forget the collective trauma many educators have experienced related to the constant back and forth of in-person and home learning during the COVID-19 pandemic and their concerns for their safety and the safety of their students.

We also have experiences outside of teaching that cause stress in our bodies, making teaching more difficult. Relationship trauma coach Lindsay Poelman shared on the Educate & Rejuvenate podcast that she often sees clients facing betrayal trauma from infidelity and divorce (Poelman & Sorenson, 2023). Her clients also face traumas from setbacks such as financial insecurity or even the loss of a pet.

Some people invalidate their suffering because they believe others suffer more. You don't have to invalidate yourself simply because you think others have it worse. The stress response your body creates is still accurate. We also have to consider that our stress response is not strictly logical. One person could handle a perceived "more difficult" situation and be more regulated than someone with a "more minor" situation, depending on their window of tolerance. In any case, invalidating our own suffering prevents us from being able to support others fully. Comparison is not helpful in this situation and may prevent you from validating yourself and getting the support you need.

It is essential to be mindful of any trauma in your body and recognize if it is something you need extra support in resolving. Bessel A. van der Kolk, author of the best-selling book *The Body Keeps the Score* explains the consequences of unresolved trauma: "We have learned that trauma is not just an event that took place sometime in the past; it is also the imprint left by that experience on mind, brain, and body. This imprint has ongoing consequences for how the human organism manages to survive in the present. Trauma results in a fundamental reorganization of the way mind and brain manage perceptions. It changes not only how we think and what we think about, but also our very capacity to think (van der Kolk, 2014)."

Our trauma may get in the way of our capacity to think, process our feelings, or apply the tools in this book. If you need more personalized support, therapies such as Internal Family Systems (IFS) and eye movement desensitization and reprocessing (EMDR) have proven to be effective in helping alleviate trauma. If you are having trouble coping with trauma, reach out to a mental health professional.

How It All Comes Together

Understanding our nervous system is the final lever that makes all the tools we've discussed so far click into place. As you learned at the beginning of the chapter, the nervous system is quite literally what creates our mind-body connection. It sends signals from the brain to the body and the body to the brain. We can't ignore one and forget the other. They are both critical.

I recently interviewed fellow life coach Leah Davidson, a former speech pathologist who now trains coaches on how to understand the nervous system, for the Educate & Rejuvenate podcast. We discussed how much we love the tools we utilize as coaches, but it isn't possible to use the self-coaching model or process our emotions if we are in a stress response cycle (Davidson & Sorenson, 2023). Our rational thinking brain goes "offline," so observing our thoughts and putting them in a model would be futile.

While we're in an activated state, it's also not quite time yet to process our emotions. While you may notice some similarities between processing emotions and regulating our nervous system, the goal behind each is different. Regulating is about bringing ourselves back into our window of tolerance and safety. Processing emotions involves fully embracing and understanding our feelings, learning to name them, and allowing ourselves to experience them completely. We need to regulate our bodies before we can process our emotions.

To make it easy to understand when to do that, Leah put the tools into a handy little step-by-step process that helps us know when to use each tool in this book.

- First, ask yourself, "Am I Safe?" With this question, you are asking yourself if you are in physical danger.
- If the answer is yes, move on to the next step. If the answer is no, get yourself to safety.
- Next, ask yourself, "Do I feel safe?
- If the answer is yes, then you can use the self-coaching model or process your emotions.
- If the answer is no, use the tools provided to regulate yourself before utilizing the self-coaching model or processing your emotions.

To regulate yourself, the first thing she recommends is to relax your body completely. Imagine yourself like a rag doll or Woody from Toy Story. Just bend over and relax. As she states on the podcast, "Stress cannot live in a relaxed body." Then, follow the other tips outlined in this chapter until you've completed the stress response cycle. Once you've completed the stress response cycle, you can move on to utilizing thought and feelings work. Until then, focus on getting regulated.

Figure 5.2
When To Use Each Coaching Tool

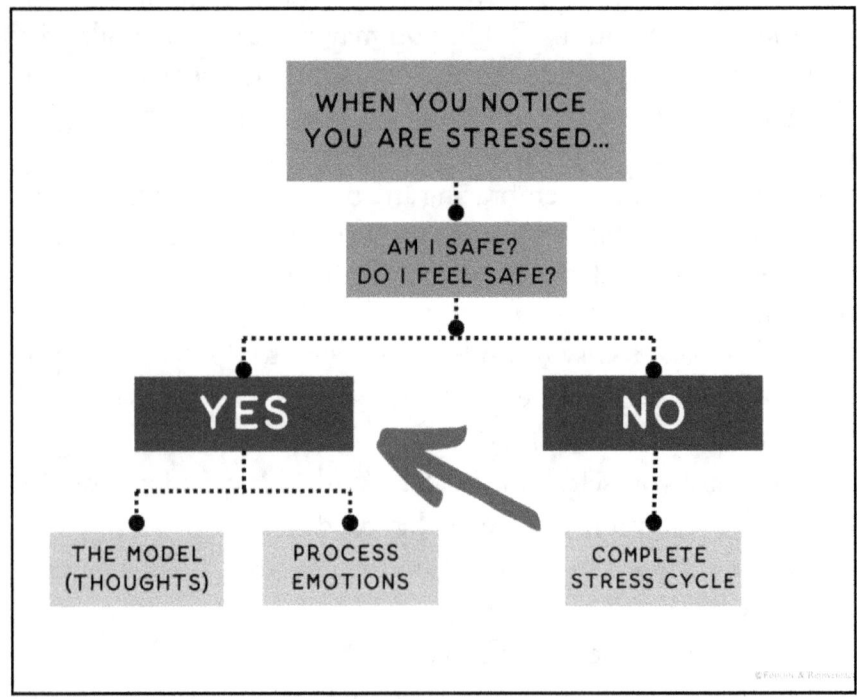

Now that you have a basic understanding of becoming an observer of your thoughts, feelings, and nervous system, you can start making conscious decisions about what you want to do with these observations. In the next section, we will continue observing ourselves and begin the next step: choosing your direction.

Step Two: Choose Your Direction

Now that you're starting to observe yourself, we can use those observations to choose what we want in our lives. We're delving deep into our psyche to truly understand ourselves and using our unique perspectives to guide choices. We're enhancing our observational skills while incorporating strategies for conscious decision-making. So, it's not "moving on" from one step to the next, but adding another layer. It's like learning to ride a bike: first, pedaling with training wheels, then balancing without losing sight of pedaling. This framework adds layers to our approach without pausing the ongoing process of self-observation.

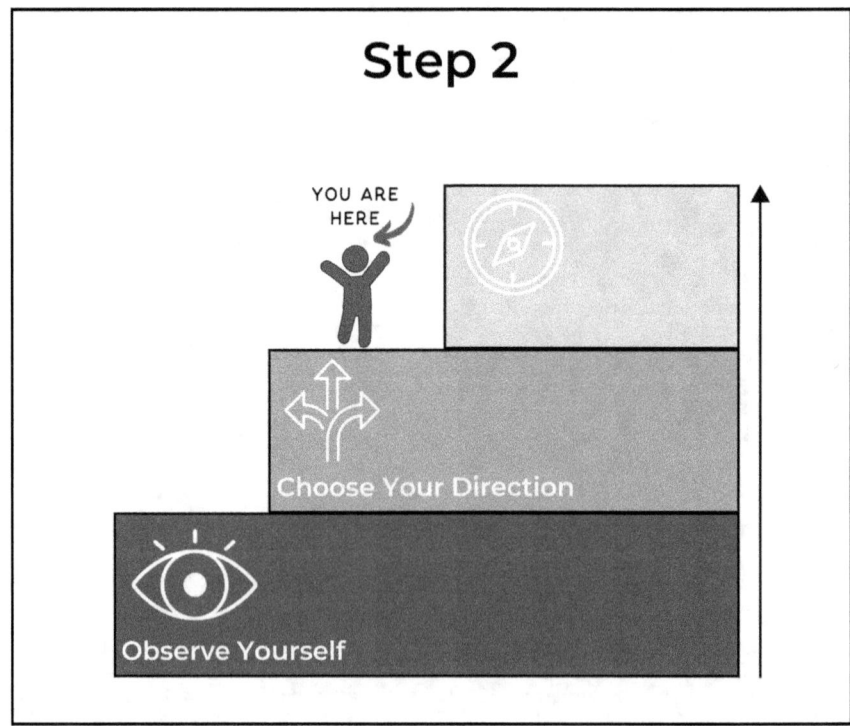

6

Taking Back Your Power of Choice

"I don't know!" uttered my blushing client for the third time after I asked her a question. Noticing her embarrassment, I assured her that she was doing great and that this was normal and part of the coaching process, because it is. Those three words are some of the most common words we hear as life coaches. Truthfully, the words "I don't know" escape my lips when I get coached, too.

This "not knowing" what we want is all too familiar. Many of us go about our lives like Rachael McAdam's character in the movie *The Notebook* (Cassavetes, 2004). I imagine the scene when they are arguing, and Ryan Gosling's character pleads, "Would you stop thinking about what everyone wants? Stop thinking about what I want, what he wants, what your parents want. What do you want?"

She just stands there, stunned.

He repeatedly asks the question, "WHAT DO YOU WANT?!"

She says, "It's not that simple."

And it's not simple for many of us for several reasons. For one, most people aren't very conscious about observing themselves and even noticing what they are thinking and feeling at any given moment, as you may have guessed by this point in the book. But it gets even deeper than that.

Ever since we were in utero, becoming familiar with our birth mother's voice and acclimating to our native language, our lens and perspective have been shaped by our experiences. From what we eat, how we dress, the vocabulary and catchphrases we use, narratives about hard work and money, religious beliefs or lack thereof, political views, values, and the parenting style we were raised with—these things and many more leave their impact on us. Our experiences will also differ based on our race and culture, whether we are in the majority or minority groups in our area, or if we've been impacted by prejudice of race, gender, sexual orientation, etc.

All of these things are the circumstances of our lives, and as we know from the self-coaching model, we do not have control over any of these things. Still, they can shape the lens through which we see the world and have a tight hold on our beliefs and how we think. The problem happens when we bring some of these thoughts and perspectives from our programming into part of our identity that may not serve us.

If you were brought up believing that good things only come with hard work, you might be even more prone to be the teacher who finds they are the last car in the parking lot nearly every school night. You might believe that your lesson plans must be perfect and that you must prove your worth as an educator by your consistent presence. Yet, no matter how hard you try, it isn't enough.

Or, possibly, you didn't feel connected with your parents growing up. Now, you are a parent and want to give your kids everything you wish you had growing up. Perhaps you're homeschooling them, buying them all the latest gizmos and gadgets, or taking them to all the fun kid places. You drop everything immediately when they ask questions or call out your name because you want them to know you care. You don't want to let them down the way you felt let down. But you realize that in the process, you are giving all of yourself to your family and leaving nothing for yourself.

Perhaps you are struggling with your mental health or self-worth, but you haven't told a soul. Vulnerability was a sign of weakness, as you learned when you showed it growing up. You quickly learned that you never want to share how you feel because it isn't safe or because it's just "not something we do." So, getting help, whether it be a therapist, a coach, or a doctor, would be unthinkable.

Maybe it's something else entirely. But the odds are, something inside your mindset and beliefs was programmed there from outside of yourself. It's not truly part of who you are but who you think you're *supposed* to be…and that's not the same thing.

This is so prevalent because the education sphere is predominantly female. Three-quarters of U.S. educators are women, a statistic shaping our paths (Condition of Education, 2023). Despite progress, gender stereotypes linger, with women often portrayed as caregivers and men as free to pursue desires. This conditioning is evident in a 2018 European study showing men's higher self-acceptance and autonomy satisfaction (Gómez-Baya et. al, 2018). Women face lower well-being and more health issues. These dynamics deepen when intersecting gender issues with race, ethnicity, and socioeconomic status, highlighting varied challenges that educators face.

No matter our circumstances, many of us find ourselves stuck in the other roles of our lives that cause us to lose ourselves. You probably chose to be an educator because you love to help others, and that's good! But when we devote ourselves to many roles, such as teacher, parent, sibling, family member, friend, volunteer, etc., we might forget who we are outside of those roles.

Before we can choose our direction, we need to understand how we subconsciously allow others to determine our choices instead of consciously choosing for ourselves. Of course, no one can force us to do anything (that's why "other people" always go in the "circumstance" line of the self-coaching model). Still, we may be doing things a certain way because that's how it's done, we want to make others happy, or simply because we don't know any other way. As Swiss psychiatrist Carl Jung said, "The world will ask you who you are...and if you don't know....The world will tell you (Oppong, 2023)."

We Are Wired for Human Connection

We don't want to consciously give away our power of choice, but there's a reason: we need human connection. We can all acknowledge that our choices are tied to an innate desire for community, and there's nothing inherently wrong with it. We are hardwired for human connection, as the fields of interpersonal neurobiology and relational neuroscience tell us. This profound yearning for connection naturally leads us to adopt beliefs and behaviors shaped by our surroundings. It is part of our shared humanity.

In fact, community is so vital that it is one of our most essential needs. According to Maslow's hierarchy of needs, the only human requirements that overpower love and belonging are our physiological needs (air, food, water, sleep) and safety (employment, resources, and health). Once our basic survival needs are taken care of, community is the ***most*** important (Maslow, 1943).

Figure 6.1
Maslow's Hierarchy of Needs

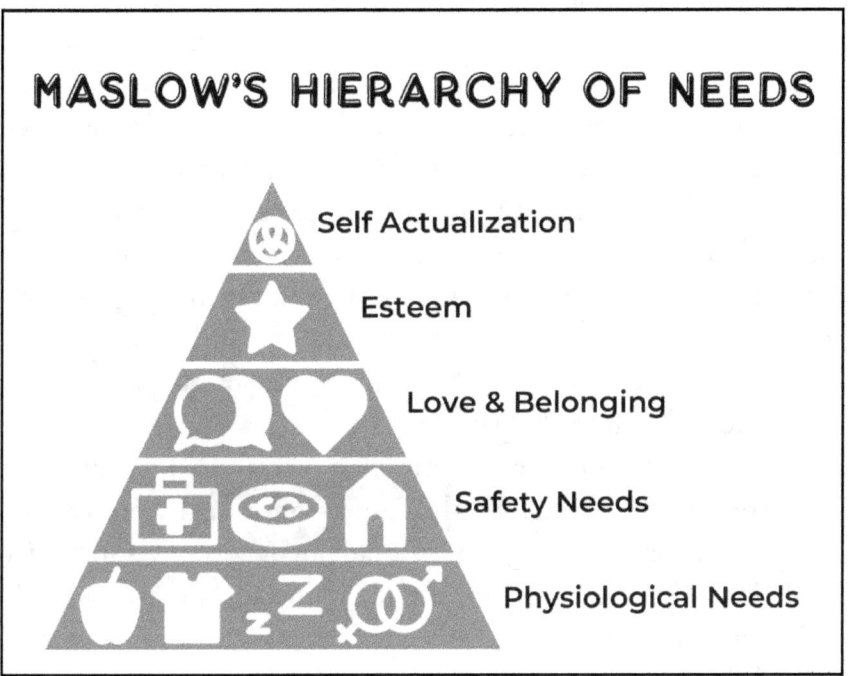

Physiological needs (air, food, water, sleep)
- Safety (employment, resources, health)
- Love and belonging (friendship, intimacy, family, sense of connection)
- Esteem (self-esteem, status, respect)
- Self-actualization (self-improvement, becoming the best we can be)

Notice that the "love and belonging" needs come *before* esteem or self-actualization, the parts about what we think about ourselves. Our connection with others comes before what we think of ourselves! This need for love and belonging is deeply embedded within our psyche. And this is a beautiful thing. Being part of a community can be one of the best ways to grow as a person. The problem arises when we become too enmeshed with others' desires and expectations at our own expense.

We often fall into the trap of believing that pleasing everyone is the key to genuine connection. In this pursuit, we inadvertently sacrifice our own authenticity, hoping it will garner more love and acceptance. As Jamie Kern Lima, renowned self-help author and founder of IT Cosmetics, shares in her book *Worthy*, "We all crave love and belonging and fear not having them. What we often don't realize is that when we're not who we truly are, we don't actually have true love and belonging anyway. It's not possible, we can have the facade of it, but it's not true, full, authentic connection when you're not participating in it authentically" (Lima, 2024).

True love and belonging can't happen when you stray from your true self. Authenticity is the cornerstone of true connection; being loved for who you truly are far outweighs any superficial validation gained from conformity or pretense. You can be both an individual and part of the whole. As you become more true to yourself, your relationships will become stronger because it won't be based on who you pretend to be. We want to belong when we let our true self shine.

Yet, breaking free from the shackles of people-pleasing, seeking external validation, and self-abandonment requires courage and introspection. It requires us to ask some tough questions, such as, *"Am I doing this for them...or am I doing this for me?"*

People Pleasing- is it for You or Me?

We *think* we people-please because we want to make everyone else happy. It sounds noble, even virtuous, because we bend backward for someone else. Helping other people is what we want to do. After all, as educators, we have big hearts and want to help; there's no denying that. But, in reality, with people-pleasing, it's not usually true that we do it to make others happy. We may not realize it, but people-pleasing is more self-serving than it seems on the surface.

Here's an example. We have a portal inside our Educate & Rejuvenate Club where our members can submit questions about their biggest struggles to be answered anonymously and asynchronously by my team of life coaches or me. Here's one of the questions a teacher submitted about when she feels conflict with her teacher team members:

"When I suspect someone is upset with me, I immediately start worrying. It takes up so much negative energy and space. Also, when we do meet to talk it over, I usually magnify the problem to where it is even bigger than it was. Any advice?"

Have you ever done something like this? I know I have. I did this last night when my husband seemed upset with me (objectively, he was shorter in his responses, spacing out, and his tone of voice sounded different than usual). However, it turns out he was just hungry (or "hangry" as many of us like to call it). We think we're good at knowing what other people want, but we are often wrong. This is the mind reading cognitive distortion.

In this case, the teacher who submitted this question thinks her coworker is upset, so she starts worrying. We don't have the full story, but we can safely assume that "magnifying the problem" means she's doing things to try to please and manipulate the situation, even when she doesn't know what this person wants or is thinking/feeling. Here is my response to this teacher:

"The first thing is what we would say in coaching is to notice that you are "getting into someone else's model" (referring to the self-coaching model from Chapter Three). This means you're not staying in your lane about the situation but getting into <u>their</u> thoughts, feelings, and actions rather than your own.

Frequently, this leads us to make assumptions, whether they are true or not (for example, they used a certain tone of voice, and we automatically assume they are upset). Maybe they are, or maybe they even tell us as such, and we aren't just guessing. But other times, we are making up situations that aren't reality inside our heads, because we don't have all the information about what is happening. Frequently, that leads to people-pleasing and unintentionally trying to manipulate or control the situation to try to "fix" it. If that is the case, this is often where we make the situation worse.

The question to think about when this comes up is... am I trying to fix this for that person's sake, or do I want to fix it so I can feel better and stop worrying? *Sometimes, it is the latter when we stop and think about it. As humans, we generally don't like feeling negative emotions."*

Usually, I answer a question in Ask a Coach and hope the person got what they needed. But this time, the teacher brought this back to a coaching call and shared that the bolded question in my response was a huge a-ha moment for her. That's when she realized she wasn't trying to stop the person from (supposedly) being upset with her so they would stop being upset. As she admitted, she wanted the person to stop seeming upset so that *she* could feel better. After all, she was feeling worried, right?

Unfortunately, it doesn't work that way. Even if the other teacher was upset at her (which we don't know for sure), she couldn't change her colleague's feelings. We can only control our own thoughts and perceptions of the situation to relieve our worry. But people-pleasing to make ourselves feel better is never the solution because we're seeking external validation.

Seeking External Validation with Our Unwritten Manuals

People-pleasing isn't the only way we seek external validation. While we make up what we think others expect us to do to make *them* happy, we also create expectations for what others need to do to make *us* happy. We don't consciously create these, or we'd realize what they are, but they are there nonetheless.

In life coaching, I was introduced to a fascinating concept called "The Manual" by my mentor, Brooke Castillo, the founder of the Life Coach School (Castillo, 2014). "The Manual" is an imaginary guide we subconsciously create for others, outlining our expectations of expressing their love for us. Strangely enough, we rarely communicate these manuals to the people in our lives, yet we hold them accountable to follow them. After all, they should know, right? They love us, and it's their responsibility to make us happy. Some examples of manuals we might have are:

- My husband should take out the trash without being asked
- That group of teachers should invite me to happy hour.
- They should teach this way or that way.
- My friends should remember my birthday.
- My principal should be softer with their feedback.
- These parents shouldn't email me so much.
- He should spend more time with the kids.
- That should have just been an email.
- My parents shouldn't be calling again.
- Customer service should respond to my email within 12 hours.
- My wife should listen to me more.
- Parents should pay more attention in the carpool drop off!
- My sister should have called me back by now.
- My brother should put down his phone when I'm talking to him.
- They should have given better gifts for Teacher Appreciation Week.
- She should help more with the homeschool co-op.
- The teacher should have given my son the part in the school play.
- My partner should watch more of the shows that I like.

This list could go on and on. Most of our manuals for each relationship we have aren't just one item like this simple bullet point list. If we were to write them down, we could probably put together a three-ring binder of our detailed, nitty-gritty expectations for others that our subconscious has created. We think that if people do these things, we can feel the love and belonging we desire.

While some experts suggest writing down and sharing our manuals with partners and then trying to do those things for each other, that is still not the healthiest approach. While it's drastically better than having an unspoken manual, it isn't ideal because you rely on someone else for validation. The other person may harbor resentment as you may expect the other person to do things they don't want to do, which may not be sustainable long-term.

We can certainly have open conversation and make requests of other people and suggest ways they can show their love—and they might be happy to oblige! We can also have boundaries. However, we don't want to tie our emotions and self-worth to whether or not someone does things the exact way we want them to. In the same way our own people-pleasing doesn't guarantee that others will be happy, we don't want to do the same thing by expecting others to do what makes us happy.

Remembering this fundamental lesson is crucial: we cannot make others happy, and they cannot make us happy. We all choose how we think and feel about our circumstances, and if we rely on what others think or feel, we create an insecure attachment as we give them all the power of what we think of ourselves. Instead, a secure attachment is the key to healthy relationships, where our validation of ourselves is independent of what others do. This is the case for our partners, our coworkers, our bosses, as well as our friends and family members.

The cases where a person should be held to a standard in the manual are limited. However, a clear and communicated set of rules and expectations is beneficial in specific contexts, such as a classroom. This ensures everyone is on the same page and understands their responsibilities. Similarly, parents may establish guidelines for household duties. As a company owner with employees, we have a handbook detailing expectations for working together. The key in any of these scenarios is that the manual is communicated and provides a structured framework for everyone involved. Even then, the point of the manual is to have clear expectations and not to put our students, children, or employees in charge of our emotions.

In most adult relationships, a manual tends to get in our way of having a healthy relationship. Loving people only when they say or do things exactly as we want isn't truly love; it's an insecure attachment. In *Atlas of the Heart*, Dr. Brene Brown shares, "The near enemy of love is attachment. Attachment masquerades as love. It says, 'I will love this person (because I need something from them).' Or, 'I'll love you if you'll love me back. I'll love you, but only if you will be the way I want.' This isn't the fullness of love. Instead, there is attachment—there is clinging and fear. True love allows, honors, and appreciates; attachment grasps, demands, needs, and aims to possess (Brown, 2021)."

So, let's shift our perspective: love isn't about control or fulfilling expectations, it's about acceptance, appreciation, and allowing each other to grow. As we navigate the complexities of relationships, let's strive to let go of attachment and embrace the freedom of genuine love.

Changing Our Unwritten Manuals

So, what can we do to change this? First, we need to understand what our subconscious, unwritten manuals contain. Get your journal (or your Educate & Rejuvenate workbook) and create a fresh page for each important relationship in your life. Write down all the expectations you can think of that would be in your manual for each relationship. Through this process, we are making the unconscious become conscious!

Then, as you analyze the list, look at the underlying needs you need to be met and ask yourself: *"What validation am I seeking, and where can I give it to myself?"* It's like the song "Flowers" by Miley Cyrus when she realizes that she can buy herself flowers and love herself better than anyone else can. What is your version of buying yourself flowers? Consider how you can show that love and compassion to yourself.

Then, you might also decide to communicate openly about what you've written in your manual. We can share as much as we'd like, which can be a great way to open ourselves up. However, any conversations we have with others should seek to understand why they do or don't do things the way we want them to, rather than trying to manipulate them into doing what we want.

If required, we can set boundaries out of love, where we kindly request what we need for ourselves and what we will do if that request is unmet. Unlike manuals, healthy boundaries promote self-responsibility and empowerment because we focus on our response rather than actions of others.

When we can love people for who they are, despite their flaws or not meeting our expectations perfectly, we are freeing ourselves of feeling the anger, frustration, or resentment that comes up when we keep our tight grip on the manuals. What would change if you let go of your manuals and instead focused only on your reactions to how others behave? It would take much less energy because while you can't control them, you can control yourself. Instead of seeking validation from others, you can put some energy into learning how to be and love the most authentic version of yourself.

The True Opposite of Selfishness Isn't What You Think.

We seek external validation through people-pleasing and because of the innate desire for love and belonging. The last thing we want to be is selfish since we deeply care about our students, families, and everyone around us. When you ask someone what it means to be "selfish," they'll often say that it's someone who puts themselves first. I decided to check if that was indeed the definition of "selfish" while preparing a podcast episode. The dictionary definition of the word "selfish" reads: "lacking consideration for others; concerned chiefly with one's own personal profit or pleasure." Selfishness is only caring about ourselves and looking out for our gain at the expense of others.

If selfishness is looking at our own gain at the expense of others, then its true opposite is looking out for everyone else at the expense of ourselves. This is called self-abandonment, and it happens when we create a pattern of neglecting or disregarding our own needs and well-being in favor of meeting the perceived needs and expectations of others. It's why we people-please and seek external validation. We have trouble saying "no" when asked to join yet another school committee. It's why we feel unfulfilled, even when we give our all, because we aren't giving our soul what it needs to be fulfilled.

If you find yourself nodding your head as you read and realize you've been self-abandoning, you're not alone. This is something that most of us have found ourselves doing. I dove into this work with my therapist and life coach by diving in internally through all my studies with my certification and beyond.

Before we can get clear about what we truly want, we also need to understand how we may have been putting what others want and need ahead of our own needs and desires. While we don't want to be selfish, we also don't want to abandon ourselves.

We want to be somewhere in the middle, and I'd argue that the "middle ground" is putting ourselves and our needs first.

You might think that sounds blasphemous, but hear me out. We may have the intrinsic desire to contribute and be part of the whole. If we are mentally, physically or emotionally depleted, we cannot do so. We can't sustainably contribute to others when it is constantly at our own expense. During one of our Educate & Rejuvenate coaching calls, my dear colleague and friend Chrissy Nichols, an executive functioning life coach for teachers, said it best: "taking care of ourselves isn't selfish. It's self-FULL (Nichols, 2023)." It allows us to fill our cups, so we have more to give to others.

We don't need to spend most of our time on ourselves (believe me, I know that wouldn't be very sustainable as an educator or a parent!). "Putting our needs first" means prioritizing whatever we need to do to fill ourselves first, similar to how when we're on an airplane, flight attendants tell adults to put on their own mask before their children's. However, first we must understand our needs and desires to do this.

Choosing to Honor Ourselves is Key

Shortly before I started my life coaching certification, I found myself grappling with what I could only describe as an existential crisis after my grandma had a stroke. She wasn't just a grandparent to me but a vital caregiver in my life. She had lived down the street from us, and we had gone to church together every Sunday. When my parents divorced when I was at the pivotal age of 12, she held me while I cried on the blue corduroy couch in our living room. Throughout that period, she cared for us while my mom embarked on a new career as a real estate agent to provide for us. Attending all my school musicals and choir concerts, she became an unwavering presence in my life, a constant source of joy. We'd spend hours laughing at dinner every Sunday as we devoured her famous Lemon Jello. Her support continued as I graduated with my elementary education degree and became a mother. The thought of losing her felt like losing a piece of myself.

The impending loss of my grandmother, the most significant one I'd faced in my life up to that point, stirred up emotions and thoughts I had repressed for over a decade. As I delved into my life coach training, these troubling thoughts and emotions lingered in the background, waiting to be fully acknowledged even as I tried to resist them.

During our training, our instructor prompted us to explore the core components of our identity and beliefs. Since this was an assignment, I could no longer ignore the fact that I found a misalignment between the answers I knew others expected and the genuine values ingrained in my soul. Do I write what I believe (the answers that come from inside of me) or what I've been told I need to think (the answers that came from what others told me to believe)?

Anger and resentment bubbled as I hesitated to write down the expected responses. I feared disappointment from those around me, even though they'd never see what I wrote. I felt trapped, believing that my own thoughts wouldn't be accepted

The problem was, now that I was studying psychology, I was onto myself. Before my studies, I was subconsciously repressing what I genuinely thought and felt. But now, I couldn't unsee how much I was fawning, people-pleasing, looking for external validation, and self-abandoning, all while putting on a happy face.

I realized that I can't ignore my needs forever if I want to do the work I feel called to do authentically. And if you're still reading the pages of this book, that means you want to do the work too—so you can't ignore your needs, either.

What feelings might you have buried deep down that are beginning to come up?

Are you still working in the same school environment where your ideas and contributions are constantly pushed aside instead of applying for other open positions?

Do you have the innate desire to start a creative endeavor but insist that it's impossible to do, so you push your creative self aside?

Have you been harboring feelings of unworthiness because of something someone else did or said to you in your past instead of realizing that you are inherently enough?

We can't keep these feelings and people-pleasing buried inside of us and get to know our true selves. We can do one or the other. We have to decide.

Choosing our direction is a process where we get clear on what *we* want in our lives: *our* pursuits in education, *our* relationships, *our* priorities, *our* values, and everything else. Dive in deep and ask yourself, "What do you want?" And by "what you want," I mean what you yearn for...if you were to take the time to dive deep down inside of yourself and decide, in a perfect world, if no one else would care or have any say or impact on what you settle on.

Exercise: What Do You Want?

What do you want? It sounds like a simple question, but as Rachael McAdams' character told us at the beginning of this chapter, it's not always that simple. But we need to understand what we truly want so we can choose our direction in our lives.

As a coach, one of the biggest lessons I've learned is that when we ask better questions of ourselves, we get better answers. We tend to focus on questions such as "what if (insert terrible thing) happens?" or "why are things not going my way?" The answers our brains find in response to questions like these often isn't very helpful in getting us where we want to go. Instead, we can focus on questions that will help our brains to focus on finding the answers.

For this exercise, I've outlined a list of questions that break down "what do you want?" into smaller, more manageable pieces. These questions will help you dive deep to understand what you truly need to thrive in every area of your life, in teaching and beyond.

- ***What is at least one thing working well in your life right now?*** Some clients can name multiple things immediately, while others struggle to name just one. This question helps us reframe our mindset before we dive into what we want to change. As we discussed with cognitive distortions in Chapter Three, it's never all or nothing.
- ***What do you love?*** To taste? To see? To touch? To feel? To hear? Tap into all five senses. Do you love warm cookies, fuzzy socks, a good cup of coffee, the smell of the rain, or the sound of the ocean? The sound of music playing on the radio? Keep writing as many things as you can. This is an easy way to get your brain connected to your body.
- ***How are you currently creating space for these things in your life?*** If you are not doing these things, what are you doing instead
- ***What parts of yourself have you let go of that you miss?*** Did you sing or play soccer as a child growing up? Did you dance to music like no one was watching? Is there any part of you that still wants to do those things now
- ***What are your top values?*** There is no right or wrong here. What is most important to you? Family? Friends? Career? Faith? Spirituality?
- ***How are these currently reflected in your life?*** Also, consider how they are not, as well.
- ***Who do you love?*** List the most important relationships in your life.
- ***Do you feel genuinely connected to each person?*** Explain why or why not.

- ***What behaviors do you notice in yourself that you do to please others? How are they keeping you from being fully yourself?***
- ***If you were to let go of these behaviors tomorrow, who would you be?*** Take a moment and describe the non-people-pleasing, authentic "you" for a moment. Visualize as you describe yourself. What do you do? How do you live? How do you hold boundaries? Explore this version of yourself now.
- ***How would becoming this version of you, your most authentic self, impact your teaching?*** Think about how you'll be able to impact the lives of the students you teach when you are coming from a place of personal fulfillment.

You'll find these questions with all of the exercises outlined in this book in the Educate & Rejuvenate Journal, which you can print out and use in any journal or notebook. You can write your initial answers but then leave room to continue adding to them. As you put your heart into answering these questions, your brain will continue seeking answers as you do your daily tasks. You'll become more and more conscious of who you are, what you need, and what you want. As you use this information to choose your direction, you'll see that living in integrity with yourself will help you feel more at peace in every aspect of your life- teaching and beyond.

7

The Power of Conscious Thinking

James had a problem: He woke up sick. His head was pounding, his throat was on fire, and he felt weak as he limped around like a zombie from *The Walking Dead*. He'd call in sick without a second thought if he worked at any job besides teaching. He daydreamed about what that would be like if he worked a desk job, just to make one quick call and not worry about what was happening at the office. He'd kick back, pop some Nyquil, and binge-watch Netflix until he passed out.

Sick days sounded like a dream…but one he could not have for himself. He'd have to put together a full day of sub plans for his fifth-grade class, which was even more challenging than going to work sick. He remembered the massive shortage of substitute teachers, so even the thought of taking a day off pained him with guilt.

This common phenomenon is one I've seen play out over and over. Over the past decade, we have received various comments when we promote our Ready To Go Sub Plans on social media. Some raved about the freedom they gave them to take a day off whenever needed, while other teachers commented that the product was useless because teachers can't ever take a day off. Isn't that interesting?

Sure, some schools have different policies regarding what your plans should look like or what percent of staff can take a particular day off, and the number of subs available will differ by area. Some principals may support you taking a day off more than others. All of this is true and would be part of the "circumstance" line of the self-coaching model.

But it's also true that an employer cannot legally deny an employee from ever taking a sick day. So why do some teachers believe they cannot take a day off, even if they are popping ibuprofen or wearing sunglasses, because they are teaching while having a migraine, while others (even in the same school) might take a day off with a lighter case of the sniffles? This range of teacher experiences is a classic example of how what we think impacts how we feel and what we choose to do.

Our Brain Wants to Be Right (More Than It Wants Us to Be Happy)

Remember, we create more of whatever we think and focus on in our teaching and our lives. There's a reason why, and it's because of our selective attention.

For example, you're considering getting a new car and deciding between two makes/models. Suddenly, you notice these vehicles on the road more often than before you started car shopping. It's not that there are suddenly more of these cars on the road, but your brain is primed to notice it because you've been paying specific attention to them.

Our brain can't possibly interpret all the stimuli it receives all day, so it must select what receives attention and what gets filtered out. As we focus on a particular car make and model, our brain suddenly knows to focus on that more because we are giving it our attention.

Not only do we filter out information based on our surroundings, but also to confirm our own beliefs. With confirmation bias, we sometimes interpret or seek information that confirms our pre-existing beliefs and actively (not just passively) avoid or discount information that contradicts those beliefs.

Maybe you have that one coworker who just drives you crazy. Perhaps you don't like the methods they use to teach or the way they leave school sooner than you do. Maybe you think they are super disorganized. You think they are a terrible teacher or a nasty coworker. Or if it's not someone at school, perhaps one of your children or your brother-in-law has been driving you up the wall lately.

Well, guess what? Your brain wants to continue to prove itself right. It will keep looking for evidence of their obnoxious behavior while completely ignoring anything else they do that doesn't align with your thinking (like if they do something nice). So, it'll look for everything this person is doing wrong and not pay attention to what this person is doing right.

Similarly, when thinking about past events, we also have selective memory, meaning that we recall or remember information that aligns with our existing beliefs, attitudes, and preferences while downplaying or leaving out the rest. Neuropathways are formed in our brains due to repeated thoughts, emotions, and behaviors. Our brains like to stick to their existing beliefs.

Even if evidence is brought to us that proves our thinking wrong, we will fight against it. In the book *Mistakes Were Made (But Not by Me)*, social psychologists Carol Tarvis and Elliot Aronson wrote, "Most people, when directly confronted by evidence that they are wrong, do not change their point of view or course of action but justify it even more tenaciously. Even irrefutable evidence is rarely enough to pierce the mental armor of self-justification (Tarvis & Aronson, 2020)."

Our brains want to prove themselves right, even if there is evidence to the contrary, and even if it is to our detriment, such as not taking a day off to take care of ourselves or making a relationship with someone we see every day unbearable (which is miserable for us and may not even affect that person).

If we are so focused on what we don't like or don't want, we create a feeling that causes us to take actions that generate more of what we don't like. The neuropathways we have built over time are powerful, so the only way to change them is to start observing ourselves. As we become more conscious, we can correct our misguided thoughts with new ones. As Supreme Court Justice Robert H. Jackson said in 1948, "I see no reason why I should be consciously wrong today because I was unconsciously wrong yesterday (Liptack, 2014)." Once we become aware of where our current thinking is not serving us, we can think more consciously to drive the feelings, actions, and results we want in our lives.

Intentional & Unintentional Models

When we are not aware of our thoughts and feelings, our brains default to an unintentional model. Through the five-step self-coaching framework, you'll learn how to use intentional models. What's the difference?

- **Unintentional Models:** The unintentional models are already happening based on thoughts that our brain thinks subconsciously. Many of these unintentional models are based on common cognitive distortions. Because they are subconscious, our selective memory and confirmation bias are hard at work. Uncovering these unintentional models through coaching (whether self-coaching or with a life coach) can help you find what's in your way of living your best life

- **Intentional Models:** Intentional models are conscious. We are using these models to choose a deliberate thought to think about a situation and determine what might happen ahead of time.

Most of the time, we are using unintentional models: we believe whatever we think. Whether we know it or not, our unintentional thoughts create our actions and results. To illustrate this point, let's circle back to James and his predicament of waking up sick and convincing himself there is no way he could take a day off. Here is what James' unintentional model might look like:

> **Circumstance:** There are 32 substitute teachers available in our district.
> **Thought:** I can't take a day off because we don't have subs.
> **Feeling:** Defeated.
> **Actions:** I don't prepare sub plans. I go to school sick. I feel resentful that I don't get to take a day off. I get upset when coworkers take a day off.
> **Result:** I don't take a day off.

Now, there is nothing wrong with James thinking these thoughts. They show some of his core values. For example, he cares about others, since he doesn't want to inconvenience others with his day off. He takes his job seriously—otherwise, he wouldn't worry about any potential consequences if a substitute teacher wasn't found. However, it's not the circumstance keeping James from taking a day off but his thoughts *about* the circumstance. And we know that this thought isn't helping him rest and recover from his illness.

We know it's the thought, not a circumstance, causing this result because other teachers take days off. Let's take another teacher in the building. We'll call her Stacey. To her, she's earned those sick days and has a right to use them. She makes it easier for herself to take a day off than to call in sick. She has a sub tub, full of Ready to Go Sub Plans she didn't even have to make herself, already prepped and ready to go. When she wakes up sick, she might immediately think, "I guess it's time to use those sick days I've earned!" She knows there is a sub shortage, but she's thinking differently about it and believes it will all work out.

This is what Stacey's unintentional model might look like:

Circumstance: There are 32 substitute teachers available in our district.
Thought: I can use the sick days I've earned.
Feeling: Confident.
Actions: I have prepared sub plans ahead of time so they are ready for a sub. I make a plan with my team on what we will do for each other when there isn't a sub. I decide ahead of time to take a day off when needed. I take a day off.
Results: I am rested and using the personal days benefit of my job.

Because Stacey's thoughts, feelings, and actions are different, we know that James' "not being able to take a day off" is a thought, not a circumstance.

However, that doesn't mean that James can necessarily flip a switch and suddenly think just like Stacey. Before he can do anything else, he needs to see and understand his current unintentional model. That's why I didn't teach about intentional models back in Chapter Three when I first taught you the model. First, we want to understand why this is happening in the first place.

James likely doesn't realize that the thought (not the circumstance) that he can't take a day off makes him feel defeated.

Put simply, James doesn't take a day off because he believes he can't. And because of this belief, he doesn't take any steps to prepare that would make it easier to take a day off if he gets sick. Once he realizes what's happening, he can change his thought model.

To shift his mindset around taking a day off, he would need to see what different thoughts might resonate with him. If he were working with me as a coach, I would ask him what other thoughts he could think about this, and I may even offer a few suggestions he could try. However, it has to be a thought that works for him. Trying new thoughts can be like trying on a piece of clothing. Some will fit some people perfectly, while it doesn't quite fit for others. Maybe he'd land on a thought like, *"I am learning that it is okay to take a sick day."*

From there, we can start an intentional model from this new thought. The difference between the original unintentional model and this new intentional one is that we chose a thought intentionally rather than it simply happening. Here is what his intentional model might look like.

> **Circumstance:** There are 32 substitutes available in our district.
> **Thought:** I am learning that it is okay to take a sick day.
> **Feeling:** Open.
> **Actions:** I start putting together a sub binder and sub plans. I ask coworkers about what it was like taking a day off. I start thinking about the possibility of taking a day off the next time I get sick.
> **Result:** I am open to taking a sick day when ready.

This is the power behind creating intentional models! Let's look at one more example. Homeschool mom Tasha wants her craft and homeschool supplies to be more organized. Here is what her model might look like:

> **Circumstance:** I have a goal to clean my cabinets, pulling out items to keep or eliminate.
> **Thought:** I might need this again someday.
> **Feeling:** Scarcity.
> **Actions:** I keep most of my supplies. I only get rid of a few things. I ruminate about what to keep and what not to keep. I keep the box of stuff I was going to take to the thrift store in the cabinet because I still haven't decided what I'm going to give away. I procrastinate. I do something else.
> **Result:** I don't have clean cabinets today.

Isn't it fascinating? By worrying that she might need the things again "someday," she is preventing herself from having what she wants *right now*, which is to have a clean craft room and homeschool space. What if she could believe that if she needed that item in the future, she could get it? Homeschool parents, like all educators, are resourceful. We can find what we need when we need it.

Let's see what would happen if she thought along those lines, keeping our circumstance line the same, and see what might change:

> **Circumstance:** I have a goal to clean my cabinets, pulling out items to keep or eliminate.
> **Thought:** I don't need this right now, and I'll figure it out if I need it later.
> **Feeling:** Abundant.
> **Actions:** I get rid of that item. I add more items to the box. I fill up the box and get another one to fill up. I take those boxes to the thrift store. I find some containers to start organizing the emptier space.
> **Result:** I am creating more room for what I want in my space and my life.

See how the result always ties back to what we think, rather than the situation? These models also show the difference between abundance and scarcity, which can appear in many ways. When we are feeling scarcity, we are more likely to react out of fear and not make decisions that align with what we want. When we feel abundant, we can make a choice that's in line with what we want to create since we believe we will always be able to find what we need.

Notice how a shift in our perspective can make all the difference. As Oprah Winfrey once said, "What you focus on expands, and when you focus on the goodness in your life, you create more of it (Kukolic, 2017)." Shifting just one thought to a more intentional one can give us the momentum to change our direction.

How do we move from an unintentional model to an intentional one? First, we need to clearly identify our unintentional model by observing our thoughts and behaviors. Remember the strategy from Chapter Three, where we do a thought download to capture our thoughts, then identify the most impactful one and build a model around it? Once we've done that, we can shift our perspective and find a new, believable thought. However, it's important to approach changing our thoughts the right way, as there is a correct and incorrect method for doing so.

The Right Way to Shift Our Thoughts & Create New Thinking Patterns

Recently, I coached a client. We'll call her Heather. She said something along the lines of, "I'm the type of person who does everything for everyone besides myself. I'm teaching, running after-school programs, and practically raising my grandbabies. So after school, I just pass out. I'm done. So I can't work out, and I don't make healthy meals. I'm so overweight. I don't have the energy to chase my grandbabies because my body is so terrible."

I replied, "First, let's have so much compassion for you right now. Look how many wonderful things you are doing and helping others. I would say it is a lot. I could argue that it is a thought that it's 'a lot,' but it doesn't always make sense to go down that route. It's not always helpful when so much more is happening here. You seem concerned about not caring for yourself, particularly your weight. You said your body is terrible. Is it true that your body is terrible, though?"

She said, "Well, right now it is. It's in the worst shape I've been in my entire life." Do you see what's happening here? She believes that her body being horrible is a fact. But from the self-coaching model, we know this is not a circumstance because it is up to interpretation.

Knowing this client was familiar with the model, I explained, "If we were to look at the model, where would it go?" Her expression showed me that she knew what I was pointing out. "It would be a thought, right? Because if I were to look at my thoughts, I'd disagree with you. In my opinion, no one's body is ever horrible. Your body is just your body."

As we continued her conversation, we observed several of her thoughts. The common theme was that she wanted to lose weight to have more energy to play with her grandbabies, but she felt like she didn't have the time for it. However, we realized that her stress about this was causing her to avoid her emotions by heading to her pantry to get a snack. So, we started questioning the thought that she didn't have time to lose weight. What if it was as simple as feeling her emotions instead of heading to the pantry?

By the end of the call, she was able to start believing that she could do something to take care of herself. However, we didn't do that by trying to immediately shift her thoughts from *"my body is horrible"* to *"I look smoking hot"* or from *"I am a person who never takes care of myself"* to *"I can spend hours on self-care."* Those wouldn't have been believable for her, so they wouldn't have worked. Instead, we found new, believable thoughts to help her head in the right direction.

Deliberate thoughts are choices, but we can't decide to have any thought we want and immediately believe it. Our current subconscious thought patterns have likely had years to take root in our minds, so we can't expect to be able to reprogram these thoughts overnight. Retraining our brains to use thinking patterns to serve us better will take time and practice. However, you can expect to see incremental improvement and success along the way as you apply these tools. The goal is to create new neuropathways with repetition.

Switching to a new thought is not just flipping the switch to the "perfect" thought. Instead, it is about taking baby steps in the right direction. To do this, you can choose a thought you can currently believe right now that is a step up from your recurrent negative thought. When you come up with a new thought that you'd love to believe in and live from, but you aren't there just yet, bridge and ladder thoughts can be an incredible way to bridge the gap between wanting to believe something and actually believing it.

Bridge Thoughts

A bridge thought is an "in-between" thought that builds a bridge between your current thought pattern and the new belief you'd like to have. These bridge thoughts should be ones that you can work towards believing. The first one should be a thought that you can believe right now, and then you'll work your way up to the belief you want to have. Some sentence starters for bridge thoughts include:

- I am learning that...
- It is possible that...
- I am becoming a person who...
- Maybe...

- I'm seeking evidence that....
- I'm open to...
- I'm considering...

You can use these sentence starters to help you find a thought that is easier for you to believe. For example, let's say you want to train for a marathon. Yet if the most you've ever run is a 5k, you might not immediately believe you could do it. Instead, you might choose to think, *"It's possible that I could train for a marathon."* That thought could be the bridge to bring you to your desired thought: "I can run a marathon."

Figure 7.1
Bridge Thoughts

Bridge thoughts are ideal when we can find a beautiful intermediate thought that we can fully believe, and it can bring us to the perfect thought. However, there are times when we need more than one intermediate thought. That's why we may need to try ladder thoughts.

Ladder Thoughts

Ladder thoughts serve a similar purpose to bridge thoughts; however, instead of one thought to build a bridge between the two, we devise a series of thoughts we can work towards believing. This can be useful when even a bridge thought doesn't seem attainable or if you need even more support as you work towards a new belief. We can work our way up in small increments as we get closer to the ideal thought.

Let's say you are struggling to believe you are worthy of love. If you struggle with feelings of unworthiness and self-loathing, that is a bit deeper in your psyche and could require baby steps towards self-love. Here is an example of what a ladder thought might look like:

Figure 7.2
Ladder Thoughts

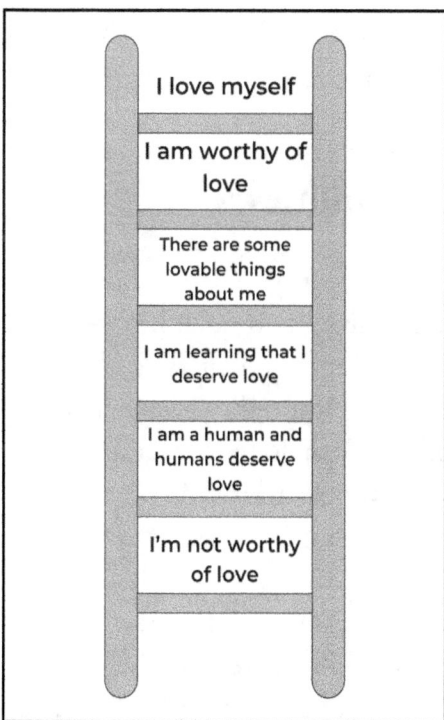

I'm not worthy of love.
I am a human and humans deserve love.
I am learning that I deserve love.
There are some lovable things about me.
I am worthy of love.
I love myself.

As you progress up the ladder, you'll get closer to your ideal thought. In the meantime, your perspective will shift, and you'll begin to feel better.

The process of utilizing either ladder or bridge thoughts will look different for everyone, but as you start looking for evidence for each thought, you'll be able to retrain your neuropathways. Keep in mind that your current neuropathways were built over time, and so your new ones will take time as well. Have patience in the process. The complete transformation we want to see doesn't happen overnight, but we can feel the weight lift off us even with a slight perspective shift, giving us a taste of what is truly possible.

Seeing the Possibilities

By now, hopefully, you are seeing the possibilities that arise when we can utilize the model, bridge thoughts, and ladder thoughts to kick our limiting beliefs to the curb. When we can consciously choose our thoughts, the magic begins to happen! Suddenly, we realize we can do so much more than we ever thought possible with the power of our minds.

Maybe your dream is to work just 40 hours a week as a teacher while still delivering top-notch lessons.

Maybe you dream of spending more time with your family while traveling the world and creating memories.

Maybe you dream of starting a side hustle, such as starting

a Teachers Pay Teachers store, launching a podcast, writing a book, or sharing some of your knowledge by creating an online course. Maybe you want to cultivate a beautiful home environment that rivals Chip and Joanna Gaines.

Once you're able to recognize what those desires are, you can utilize the power of your conscious thoughts to help you reach your goals, no matter what they are. In the next chapter, you'll learn how to create goals that align with your true desires and develop an action plan to help you get closer to them, one step at a time.

8

Choosing Your Dreams & Goals

It was a moment four years in the making. After years of studying life coaching and dreaming of becoming a coach, I was finally about to join a Zoom call that would determine if I'd become officially certified after taking the final exam. For life coaches, this is the equivalent of a teacher's final observation and the Praxis exam needed for certification.

In our certification program, we had a practicum in addition to the training. To prepare for my final call, I decided to use my final practice call right before my official one. However, when the time came I was so "in my head" about doing everything right that I got flustered. If it had been the official call, I wouldn't have passed. I hung up with a lurch in my stomach and feeling an impending sense of doom, knowing I'd be face to face with the same instructor again, wanting her to certify me in just one hour.

So what did I do? I remembered that I was completing a certification as a *life coach*—and that one of the incredible tools I had been mastering was the self-coaching model. And I knew the result I wanted...to certify on my next call.

I got out a pen and paper and wrote the letters C, T, F, A, and R down the page (for "Circumstance," "Thought," "Feeling," "Action," and "Result"), But instead of starting with the "Circumstance" line of the model, I started a model with the "Result" line, like this:

C:
T:
F:
A:
R: I passed my call, and I am a certified life coach

Then, I put the "Certification Call" in the "C" line, since that call on my calendar was a fact. Then I asked myself, *"What actions must I take to certify as a coach?"* Finally, I wondered what I'd need to think to feel that way. Here is what the model looked like:

C: Certification Call
T: I am ready
F: Confident
A: Enter the call with curiousity, ask open ended questions, pick a T, get a clear C, make sure the C+T match, if they match ask what they do and don't do when they feel that way, clarifying if it doesn't seem right, if stuck ask what they do if they didn't feel that feeling, let the result reveal itself, make sure to deliver it confidently, stay curious about the model and not worry about if I'm passing, breathe & redirect if my mind wanders
R: I passed my call, and I am a certified life coach

Figure 8.1
Self Coaching Model on Sticky Note

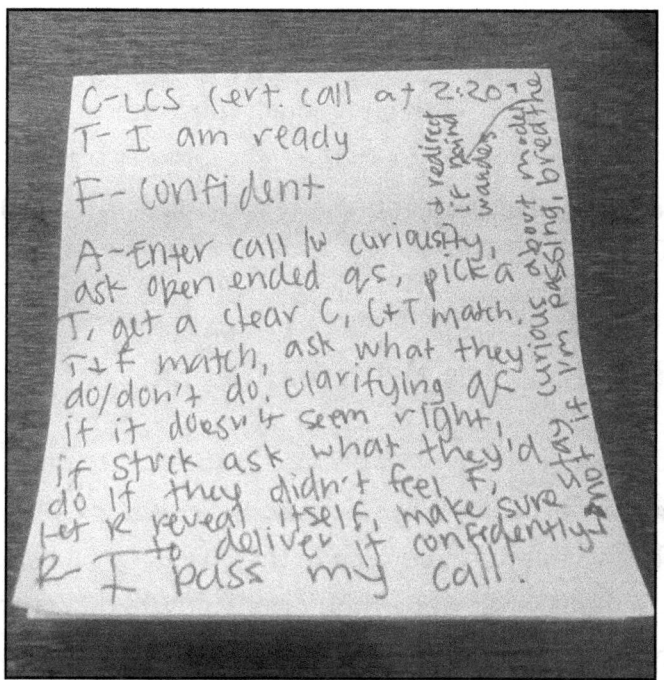

My energy completely shifted. I had the roadmap, precisely what I needed to do to succeed. Even though just 15 minutes prior, I had done the exact opposite things, I knew it was because I was not living according to this intentional model. I had been stuck in an unintentional model that was guided by my thought of "I might not pass" that led to fear. So of course, fear didn't lead me to take the right actions to certify. But once I created the intentional model above, I could tap into the feeling of confidence instead. I brought that energy into the call and certified it with flying colors.

Since then, I've used the self-coaching model backward whenever there is a desired result that I want to see. There is a reason that utilizing a model like this works. In his book *Be Your Future Self Now*, Dr. Benjamin Hardy says, "Decisions and actions are best when reverse-engineered from a desired outcome. Start with what you want and work backward. Think and act from your goal rather than toward your goal (Hardy, 2022)."

But before we can do that, there's a process we need to follow. First, we want to understand why we set goals in the first place (it's not because we aren't "enough" now or because it'll make us happier). We want to get in the right mindset before creating our goals out of a place of abundance and then create a plan to set ourselves up for success.

The Two Reasons We Create Goals

We don't create goals because we think reaching the goal will make us happier. Why? Because we've learned throughout this book, it's not the circumstance that makes us happy, but our thoughts about where we are. You can cultivate the feelings you want to have right now, and you are already whole and worthy, just as you are in this moment. You don't have to change a thing about yourself for all of this to be true.

If you've been working towards being more accepting of yourself and living in the present moment, you might worry that your goals will pull you out of that. You might think it'll send you back into hustle mode or push your happiness off to some future goalpost. Is it possible to embrace the present fully while creating goals for the future? The answer to that question is a resounding "yes!" when you follow the process outlined in these pages. There are two reasons we set goals, and neither of them is because we want to change ourselves or that we'll be happier when we achieve them.

Reason #1: Goals Help Us Remove Our Subconscious Blocks We Have About Ourselves

The first reason we set goals is to remove any blocks that keep us from realizing how wonderful and capable we already are. It's not as much about reaching the goal but about believing that we can do what we set our minds to. Instead of focusing on everything we lack as we set our goals, we want to focus on how far we've come.

A concept I love is "The Gap and The Gain" by Dan Sullivan, the founder of Strategic Coach, and explained in detail in his book collaboration with Dr. Benjamin Hardy under the same title (Sullivan & Hardy, 2021). It highlights two ways to view progress: focusing on how far we've come or how far we still need to go. The goal remains the same, but our perspective changes everything.

"The Gap" is when we constantly compare ourselves from where we are to the continually moving goalpost of where we "want" to be. When we are in "The Gap," we will feel a lot of resistance as we try to move towards our goals, since it tends to create emotions such as failure, frustration, disappointment, and guilt.

"The Gain" is when we compare where we are to how far we've come. We still want to achieve a goal, but our happiness isn't tied to it. We notice all our gains, and we're optimistic about our ability to reach the next goal, without tying our happiness or self-worth to achieving it. Feelings we tend to feel in "The Gain" include success, satisfaction, enjoyment, and confidence.

In the book, Hardy explains that ambitious, high achievers are most prone to finding themselves in "The Gap." From my experience working with thousands of educators who always want to put their best foot forward, I'd put educators in the "Ambitious High Achiever" category. I also know you've probably forgotten all the incredible things you have accomplished to get to wherever you are.

Just think of everything you had to do from the moment you began until now. Think about it this way. At one point, you wanted to become an educator, and now here you are! And if you are at the beginning of your education journey, you might think, *"I haven't done any of those things yet! I haven't made any progress."* You're reading this book right now, right? That is making progress! What else have you done? I bet there's a lot more than you think.

The reality is you are at a goalpost you once set. You just forget to stop and think about how far you have come. Or you might think it doesn't matter. It wasn't that good, because this other thing is better. But that's not true! If you could come that far and currently stand where you once wanted to be, then who's to say you can't get from here to a new goal? This will allow you to bust through those subconscious blocks that keep you from realizing your capabilities.

The difference when we set goals from "The Gain" is that we are not setting goals from a place of lack. By setting goals while utilizing this mindset, we can work on those subconscious blocks that keep us in "The Gap." It allows us to notice when we fall into "The Gap" and shift ourselves into "The Gain." We can tap into the feelings as if we are already there because we believe in ourselves and our capabilities.

As we think of how far we've come and shift into "The Gain," we have an abundant mindset, leading us to feel good and making it easier to take the actions necessary to reach our goals. As Dr. Benjamin Hardy states, "If you focus on what you lack, you lose what you have. If you focus on what you have, you gain what you lack (Sullivan & Hardy, 2021)."

Reason #2: Goals Are Our Guide as We Choose Our Direction

The second reason we set goals is that they help us choose the direction we want to go, which is an essential step of the overarching framework for this book. It gives our selective attention something to focus on, rather than our attention being focused on whatever our subconscious brain will focus on if we don't set goals.

If our brain is thinking thoughts and focusing on certain things no matter what we do, we can use that to our advantage to get what we want in our lives. If we wish to shift and change our lives, we will. If you were to think about yourself ten years ago, would you be able to name several different things about you then versus now? While every seven years, every cell in our body is regenerated, aspects of ourselves also change.

We can visualize ourselves as three different people: our past self, present self, and future self. We tend to think of what is possible based on what our past self has (or hasn't) been able to achieve. Unfortunately, we usually use this to hold ourselves back instead of propel ourselves forward. We can't change the past, but we can tell ourselves our past is precisely what it was supposed to be and that we learned everything we need to know so we can set ourselves up for the future. We can take the gains and the lessons but then focus on the present and future.

When we set a goal, we can start aligning ourselves to who we want to be in the future. As our present self, we can tap into that energy and ask ourselves, *"What can I do today that will help my future self?"*

It's not about the end goal or making ourselves feel better. It's about the lessons we learn and the person we become along the way as we uncover the best version of ourselves that is already within us. It's similar to what Michelangelo said about his sculpture of David, "I created a vision of David in my mind and simply carved away everything that was not David (Smithsonian Associates, 2020)." Clearly, Michaelangelo was in "The Gain" mindset! We don't become better—we simply reveal what we were already capable of.

As we get clear on what we want in our lives, our goals will be our anchor that will help us see if we are going in the direction we want to go. We'll be able to refer back to them to adjust and realign ourselves as needed.

Choosing & Breaking Down Your Goals

Now that we know the healthy mindset about breaking down goals let's start, one exercise to begin with is to create a list of 25 things you want to achieve, but with a twist. I want you to write something you have already completed every other line. This mindset exercise will help you tap into abundance because you can realize that you can, and do, achieve things you want.

Once you've finished the list of 25 things you want to achieve (with half being ones you have already done), you'll want to choose just one or two that you haven't yet reached to become your main focus goals. I recommend focusing on no more than two goals at a time: one personal and one work-related (or if you want to put all your focus into one, you can get even more focused). This is so we can put our complete focus on those goals. If you set too many goals, you'll divide your attention so much that you'll struggle to meet them.

1) Ask Yourself the Following Questions:

What is the goal I want to reach? Get clear and specific about what the outcome will look like. You can take a whole page to fill it out with all the details. You want to know exactly when you will reach this goal.

Why do I want to achieve this goal? It's essential to know the why behind the goal. It could be as simple as it sounds.

How do I feel when I imagine reaching this goal? Close your eyes and imagine your feelings when you reach your goal. Tap into the emotion and feel it right now. What does it feel like? Write it down.

What will be the same when you reach this goal? This will help us realize that it is neither better here or there. Either way, we have the human experience with our human emotions, which will be optimistic about half the time, and negative about half the time. This question helps us recognize how we are already in alignment with the goal, which will ease resistance.

What will be different when you reach this goal? Imagine your future self who has already reached your goal. What do they do differently? What circumstances have changed? Write down anything that comes to mind.

2) Work the Self-Coaching Model Backwards for Your Goal

As I did at the beginning of this chapter, I want you to work the model backward, starting with the result. Write Result, Actions, Feelings, Thoughts, and then the Circumstance vertically on your page. Like this (but leave at least a few lines between each one so you have room to write):

Result:
Actions:
Feeling(s):
Thought(s):
Circumstance:

Then, you will start with the "R" line and write the desired result. Next, fill in the "Circumstance" line, which will be something like "I have set a goal to _____." In between, fill in the actions, feelings, and thoughts you will need to have.

Result: What will you see when you reach this goal?
Actions: What actions do you need to take to get this result?
Feeling(s): What feeling(s) do you need to have to take these actions without resistance?
Thought(s): What thoughts do you need to think this way?
Circumstance: "I have set a goal to _____" (fill in the blank).

Now, you know the exact roadmap you need to follow to think, feel, and do what you need to do to reach your goal

3) Turn Obstacles into Strategies

We often set goals, but something gets in our way, and we give up. That's because we didn't plan for the obstacles. So, what you'll want to do next is write down everything you can think of that might get in the way of reaching your goal. Then, for each obstacle you write down, you'll want to devise a way to overcome it. We're essentially turning your list of obstacles into a list of strategies that will help you stay on target! Since you made decisions ahead of time, your brain will know what to do when each obstacle arises instead of automatically giving up.

4) Create Tiny Tasks & Deadlines

Looking at one big goal can feel daunting. For example, if you're writing a book, want to lose 70 pounds, or train for a triathlon, you're not going to reach that goal overnight. We may also procrastinate on our goal, saying "we don't know" what to do next. It can take a lot of energy to make constant decisions if we're figuring it out as we go.

Instead, we will break down our goal into every single step we need to take between now and when the goal is reached. This will help us see progress sooner, which will help us to gain momentum and make it easier to stick to it since we already know what to do next. Break your goal down into tiny tasks and assign a deadline to each one, which will give you a timeline for reaching your goals, including when you want to complete the goal at the end, as well. You'll need to be able to tell exactly when you've reached the goal. You can adjust these later as necessary, but this will help you become accountable to yourself.

5) Creating Strong Habits

As James Clear says in his New York Times Bestseller *Atomic Habits*, "You do not rise to the level of your goals. You fall to the level of your systems (Clear, 2018)." We can set goals all day long, but if we don't create sustainable, actionable habits that help us bring those goals to life, we will work against resistance.

Consider what habits that, if you could sustain them, would

make reaching your goals feel effortless. Then, figure out how to stack these habits on top of each other. When you stack one habit on top of another (for example, after I do X, then I'll do Y), you create a system you can depend on. Over time, these habits will make it much easier for you to reach your goals. According to Clear, when it comes to habits, we can "Never miss twice." This is because "missing once is an accident, missing twice is the start of a new habit."

6) Celebrate

We want to celebrate all along the way! We can start by celebrating when we have created a complete plan with the reflection questions, self-coaching model, obstacles and strategies, and habits listed out. Then, utilizing the list of tiny tasks and deadlines, devise a way to celebrate as you mark off each one.

You'll also want to come up with a BIG way to celebrate once you've reached the goal. While not required, it is even more fulfilling if the celebration can relate to achieving the goal. For example, if you want to lose weight, you could set aside some money to buy yourself new clothes when you reach your goal.

Goal Setting Process in Action

I want to set you up for success with this process, and it helps to see a real-life example. One of my clients, who we'll call Rebecca, wanted to get her house organized during the summer. Here's what that looked like following my goal-setting process:

Rebecca's Goal: Organize House During the Summer

1) Reflection Questions

What is the goal I want to reach? I want to get my house clean and organized during the summer.

Why do I want to achieve this goal? I want to invite people to my house and feel pride in my home. I want a clean environment where there are always places for people to sit when they come over that aren't covered in piles.

How do I feel when I imagine reaching this goal? I will feel proud of myself and like a burden has been lifted. I feel much more at peace in a clean environment.

What will be the same when you reach this goal? I will live in the same house and love my home and neighborhood. It will be full of beautiful memories and family who I love.

What will be different when you reach this goal? I will have better cleaning habits that I hope to maintain to keep a cleaner environment once I'm done. I will probably invite people over much more often!

2) Working the Self-Coaching Model Backwards

R: I have a clean, organized home without piles everywhere.
A: I create a plan for cleaning; I deep clean once a week; I make time to tidy every day; I don't make excuses for not doing it; I pick up so the floor can be vacuumed by robot each day; I figure out where to store each of the things that normally end up in piles; I get whatever containers I need to organize; I get rid of stuff I don't need.
F: Determined
T: I am becoming a person who has a clean home
C: I have set a goal to create a clean, organized home

without piles everywhere.

3) Turning Obstacles Into Strategies

My biggest obstacle is that I don't want to clean when I don't have energy. My solution is to either go for a walk outside or ride my exercise bike each morning, since I've noticed that I have more energy when I move my body in the morning.

4) Tiny Tasks & Deadlines

I want to have the deep cleaning (mopping, scrubbing baseboards, etc.) done before summer school begins. Then, I want to finish the organization for the remainder of the summer.

(Note: To create the full plan, she would list each part of her "deep cleaning" with a deadline and each area of her house that needs to be organized. She'd also list anything she needs to buy (such as containers for organizing or decor) and when she wants to take a trip to the thrift store to donate items. Her deadline for the whole goal is by the last day of summer, and she will know this is complete when there are no more piles on any on the flat surfaces and everything has its place).

5) Creating Strong Habits

Here are the habits I will create for my goal:

- Riding my exercise bike or going for a walk each morning.
- Doing my daily tidying up immediately after exercise.
- Weekly rotating deep cleaning or organization tasks, which I

will do every Tuesday after exercise.
- Create a new habit of picking up five things every time I get a drink of water and after meals.
- Before bed, I will:
    - Clean up all flat surfaces and piles.
    - Ensure the floor is tidied so the robot vacuum can get to the floor.
    - Mark on my habit tracker once I have completed these things and write my streak number on a sticky note on my bathroom mirror.

Note: Notice some of the cueing, habit stacking, and tracking she is doing with these habits, which will help set her up for success!

6) Celebrating

Each night, I will give my husband a "high-five" after updating the sticky note on my mirror. After I complete each of the tiny tasks on my timeline, I will text a friend who agreed to be my accountability buddy. When I finish the deep cleaning, I will treat myself to a spinning pencil organizer for my desk (the one I've been wanting to splurge on at Hobby Lobby)! When I reach the goal, I will replace the flooring in my living room and have a party in my clean, beautiful home.

Trusting the Process

Choosing to reach our goals and dreams is one of the best ways to learn more about what is possible for ourselves. Remember, reaching for our goals and dreams isn't just about achieving them. It's about what we discover about ourselves in the meantime. Even if you don't hit your goal precisely as your plan mapped out, you will learn more about yourself by going for the goal and finding yourself closer than if you'd never set the goal in the first place.

Sometimes, we'll even find that our original goal isn't where we need to go after all, but it's a starting point for choosing our direction. If that's the case, we'll know as we continue to align ourselves. As spiritual teacher Gabrielle Bernstein teaches, we can think of our goals as "this, or something better (Bernstein, 2019)." Trust the process and know that, even as unexpected obstacles and setbacks arise, you can overcome them and be stronger having done so.

Creating our plan for our goals is just the starting point. We need to keep choosing, adjusting, and aligning ourselves to make sure we keep the promises that we made to ourselves. As we work towards our goals, we'll likely face emotions that we'll need to process, or limiting thoughts and beliefs that will arise again. This is normal and part of the process that helps us learn and grow. In the final section of the book, we will continue to observe ourselves, choose again, and align ourselves with our direction.

Step 3: Align Yourself

Now that you've observed yourself, set intentions, and chosen your direction, it is time to align your inner compass. Similar to navigating a forest using a compass, this process is ongoing. Continuously check in to ensure you're headed in the chosen direction while staying true to your values and 'why.' The journey involves perpetual self-observation, assessing alignment with your chosen path, and making necessary course corrections. Embrace the inevitability of veering off course, recognizing it as a natural aspect of the human experience.

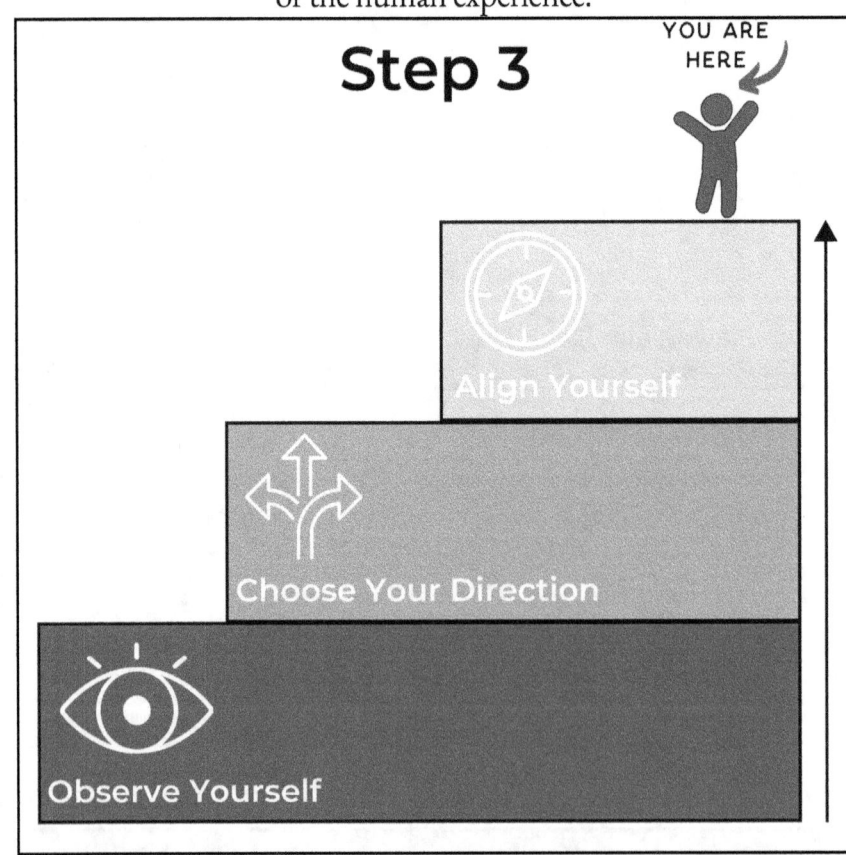

9

Getting Aligned With Your Direction

In today's world, "balance" is hailed as the ultimate life goal. We're bombarded with advice on achieving "work/life" balance through endless discussions, blog posts, and podcasts. As educators, many of us crave this elusive equilibrium, believing it would vastly improve our lives.

Yet, there's a chorus of dissent from those who argue that balance is a myth—a fleeting dream in the chaos of our daily grind. I've felt that struggle myself.

One hectic day, amidst the whirlwind of homeschooling, work, and chauffeuring my kids to various activities, a conversation in the car with my oldest son Parker triggered a revelation. His reluctance to attend his coding class made me pause and question our packed schedule. And if I'd packed my kids' schedules full with more than was necessary, chances are I'd done that in my homeschooling and business to do lists, too.

It dawned on me: I could continue trying to balance *all*

of these things, or I could take a good hard look at everything on my personal, work, and family to-do list and question what things were there that didn't need to even be balanced at all. And maybe if I actually removed some things, it would be easier to balance.

In that moment of reflection, I realized that while balance isn't entirely unattainable, it's not the complete picture either. Perhaps the real answer lies in finding a middle ground—a balance where certain obligations need not be juggled at all.

Consider this car analogy: For tires to work efficiently, they must be balanced, meaning the weight is evenly distributed. If the tires aren't balanced, then the car will get stuck. However, it's not the only thing our tires need. We could have perfectly balanced tires, but the car will still get stuck if our tires aren't aligned (meaning they all point in the right direction).

The same is true for our lives. What if we're stuck because we've *only* been focused on balance? If we haven't aligned everything in the direction of our goals, we can still feel chaotic. After all, who wants to spend equal amounts of time running in opposite directions?

This is why we also want to focus on alignment, which, like a car, is looking at the direction we are pointed. We ask ourselves, "Am I headed in the right direction in each of these important areas of my life?" This question is often the missing piece.

You'll want to look at each area in your life and whether it is headed in your chosen direction, desires, and values. Remember, we already clarified these in Chapter Six. To align ourselves to our chosen direction, we let go of any noise or expectations from others that aren't required.

This doesn't mean we let go of the idea of having a balanced life. Instead, we let it happen more naturally. As we align ourselves, we create more balance in the process because we let go of what is less critical. If we only think about balance, we aren't necessarily getting clear, just juggling everything. If we strive for alignment, we don't need to be as worried about the perfect balance because we're saying "yes" to things that matter in each category and saying "no" to some of the other noise, making what's left easier to balance in the process.

Just like a car, we want to look at balance and alignment. What most people are searching for without knowing it is alignment—getting clear on what they want. They've tried to balance themselves, but they were missing a piece. With balance alone, you are just trying to juggle more and more without looking at the *"why."* With alignment, you are getting clear on the direction and letting things go, so you are balancing fewer things. We're choosing what's important and letting go of the rest.

My Favorite Tool for Getting Aligned: A Vision Board

A vision board is my favorite tool for getting aligned. Creating a vision board can help you figure out where to align yourself in all areas of your life. Then, once you've made it, utilizing it each day will help you rewire your thinking patterns, tap into feelings you need to feel, and know when you need to adjust things along the way. Essentially, it's a tool that can help you put everything we've discussed in this book into action!

Remember earlier in the book when we discussed selective memory and how our brain filters information to prove itself? We may have goals and things we want for our lives, but if our focus is not in the right place, we will be working against ourselves. Naturally, most of us focus more on getting away from what we don't want rather than moving towards what we do want.

Figure 9.1
My Physical Vision Board

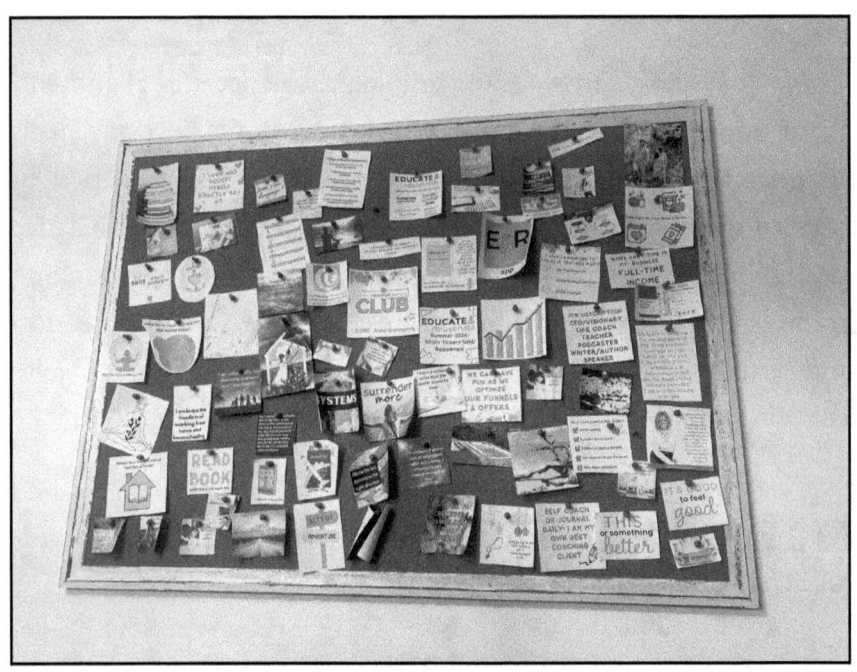

If we think, *"It's impossible to get small groups to work,"* or *"Why don't my kids ever listen to me?"* we are focused on what's not working instead of what could work. You likely know this isn't great mind-training by this point.

We genuinely want these goals and desires for our lives, otherwise they wouldn't be goals in the first place. Our more profound, conscious desire is to take those dreams and make them reality. The problem is that our subconscious brain wants to be right first and foremost. If we don't believe in ourselves or focus more on the negative, our brain will try to prove that right instead of focusing on reaching our goals.

To rewire our subconscious brain, instead of focusing on getting away from pain, we want to focus on moving toward pleasure. Our subconscious will always be along for the ride, but let the consciousness take more control. And this is where a vision board shines as a tool.

A vision board is so powerful because it allows us to see the reality we desire. Our brains respond more strongly to visual input than written input, such as to-do lists or goals. When you spend some time with your vision board each day you are training your reticular activating system (the bundle of neurons in your brainstem that regulates behavioral arousal, conciousness, and motivation) to focus on your desires (Arguinchona & Tadi, 2023).

You'll notice opportunities that you may not have before. Maybe a Facebook ad you would have scrolled past, you stop your scroll instead because the offer perfectly fits your goals, and you get the help you need. Or maybe, because you put it on your vision board, you start telling others about your goals and dreams. Someone you know has a tip to share with you. Or maybe it just helps you make better decisions throughout the day because you're reminded each day of your goals. Ideas also come when we prime our brains to prepare for them.

Do you see why this is such a powerful tool? Don't overthink it and wait until you're ready to create the "perfect" vision board. When I learned about vision boards at a conference in 2017, I started mine as soon as I got home. I found a piece of cardboard, put tin foil on it, printed some pictures, and hung it on the wall. I didn't care that it wasn't "pretty" because I didn't want to wait a single day to start. (My handy husband created a nice one a week later because he didn't like the tin foil cardboard on the wall—but I would have kept it there until I got around to making another one)! I've even made it super easy for you by adding vision board printables to the resources, which you can access here: www.teachergoals.com/educate-resources or scan the qr code below.

So, my challenge is to start yours right away, just like I did!

Creating Your Vision Board

To create a vision board, first decide whether to start with a physical or digital vision board. My preference is a physical one that I see hanging up in my bedroom every day, but some people prefer digital, and you can also do BOTH if you want to! Next, start collecting photos for your vision board. There are four things I want you to keep in mind as you plan out what content to include on your vision board:

1) Thoughts
2) Feelings
3) Actions
4) Results

You will recognize these as components of the self-coaching model! Many people use a vision board only to visualize "results," but it's an even better tool when you use it to tap into the thoughts and feelings you want to have daily that will help get you there. The great news is that by this point, you probably already have an idea of each thing you want. So now, you'll just need to devise a way to turn each concept into an image.

Figure 9.2
My Digital Vision Board

Here's an example of coming up with visuals for your vision board. Maybe your goal is to lose a certain number of pounds during the school year. Here are some possibilities of what could go in each category and how you could visualize each on your vision board:

- ***Thoughts:*** I can do this; This will be Fun; I am Strong. *Visual ideas: stylize these thoughts and put a photo to go along with each one.*

- ***Feelings:*** Motivated, Determined
  Visual ideas: Words or images that help you to feel these emotions
- ***Actions:*** I eat more vegetables. I use a 16:8 eating window for intermittent fasting. I finish a strength training program and walk each week. *Visual ideas: vegetable photo, 16:8 stylized, visual of all the days checked off of your strength training program, walking stock photo.*
- ***Results:*** I want to lose 50 pounds. *Visual ideas: mock up a scale with your goal weight on it in Canva.*

The next thing you want to plan is the type of images to include on your vision board. I've divided them into four main types:

- ***Mockups:*** You will create a visual of something that hasn't happened yet. For example, suppose you are working on a certificate to uplevel your professional career, such as an ESL endorsement or a coaching certification. In that case, you might search what the certificate from your school looks like and put your name and graduation date on it, so you can visualize it as if it's already happened.
- ***Images & Text Together:*** You can create an image for a quote, goal, thought, or affirmation. This can be a great way to both internalize and visualize new thoughts.
- ***Text Only:*** These images are text-based and can be quotes, affirmations, thoughts you want to think, or even individual words. Many people pick a "word of the year." If you're one of those people, put that word on your vision board!
- ***Simple Images:*** A picture is worth a thousand words, and a vision board is all about visual input. So, images without text can be super powerful on your vision board. (This is different than a mock-up you create as it can be just any image you grab from Google or a magazine that fits the vibe you would like).

I recommend combining these image types to add variety to your vision board. However, there is no right or wrong way to create it. The vision board is *yours!* Tap into your creativity and make it your own. You can arrange the images however you'd like.

Once your board is created, you'll want to find the right place to put it. Make sure it's somewhere you feel comfortable having it up and where you will see it regularly.

In addition to having your vision board where you will naturally see it, you'll want to create an intentional practice of looking at it each day. While making it is an excellent exercise in getting to know your goals, it isn't going to train your brain if you don't utilize it. I recommend three minutes of focused time each day. We can all make time for just three minutes for something that will help us rewire our brains, train our subconscious thoughts, and get us where we want to go. That's not much longer than brushing our teeth. Plus, you could even double up and look at your vision board while brushing your teeth if you wanted to!

During these three minutes, you will scan each picture on the board and remember what it means. Tap into the thoughts, feelings, and actions you want to take into your day. Ask yourself, *"What am I doing to create these things?"* Then, take some time to focus on one thing you are most drawn towards and think a little more about how you can intentionally create the space or search for opportunities for that visual in your life.

Have patience in the process, knowing life is always a journey rather than a destination. As you shift your mindset, you'll likely start seeing some of the items on your vision board come to life! As you do, celebrate! You can leave them on your board as gratitude and a reminder of what you've accomplished, or take the item down and put it in a notebook or journal. Then, you can start putting together a book of all of the items you have accomplished over time.

You can do the same thing if you decide to redirect and determine that a goal you've put up is no longer something you want. That in itself is a win! You are choosing a new direction again and aligning yourself with it. You can change anything on your vision board at any time. It is not meant to be a one-and-done document but a living document that changes as you go. It is also a daily reminder of what you want so you can consciously choose to create more of it and less of what you don't want.

Now, you're probably starting to see the power of adding a vision board into the tools you can use to thrive as a teacher. To make utilizing the vision board even easier, you can build time to focus on your vision board into a morning and evening routine for another quick win.

Create a Morning/Evening Routine With Minimum Baselines

I want you to have quick "wins" as you align yourself. A vision board is an incredible way to get the momentum going! You can also create a morning and evening routine aligning you with where you want to go. Instead of only having goals, you'll have systems to help you achieve your ideal life.

How many times have you said you'll start something, but then it doesn't happen? Chances are, you weren't specific about what you wanted to do and when, making it easy for you to skip it. Morning and evening routines are a great way to clarify what we want and implement habit stacking, a crucial component to creating lasting habits from James Clear's book *Atomic Habits* (Clear, 2018). He shares the "Four Laws of Behavior Change" needed to create lasting habits:

- **The Cue:** Make it Obvious
- **The Craving:** Make it Attractive

- **The Response:** Make it Easy
- **The Reward:** Make it Satisfying

Here is a process to create your routines to check all four boxes. Make a specific list of what you will do in your routine and when. Then, start with a cue for the first part of your routine. The first step of the routine will cue the rest of it (as Clear calls "habit stacking").

For example, if you want to start each morning with a workout, you can end your evening routine by putting your workout clothes and shoes beside your bed. This will be your cue to start your morning routine and follow each step to the end.

While everything in your routine should lead you in the direction you want to go, chances are there are things you want to do long-term that don't always sound "fun" in the short term. To increase your chances of success with your routine, at least one of those things should be something that you want to do in the short term, making completing the routine more desirable.

We also want to make completing the routine easy, even on the busiest days. This is where we want to make a minimum baseline for each routine step. The point of a minimum baseline is to set the bar low for what is acceptable for the habit, making success easy.

For example, this could be reading just one page of a book with your kids before bed. This minimum might feel silly or pointless. But it's not. Every little bit helps, and setting a minimum baseline helps us be consistent. Many days we'll keep going beyond the minimum baseline, but having one helps us get started and keep moving forward.

Finally, we want to make completing the habit satisfying! One of the ways we do that is by rewarding ourselves with something we want to do at the end. We can also keep track of our progress using a habit tracker. Seeing our "streak" and consistency increase makes us want to keep it going.

Here is an example of what a morning and evening routine could look like:

Morning routine:

- Put on workout clothes and shoes.
- After I put on my workout clothes, I will move my body for at least three minutes.
- After I exercise, I will meditate for at least one minute.
- After I meditate, I will look at my vision board for at least one minute.
- After I look at my vision board, I will fill up my large tumbler with water while repeating a thought I am training myself to think.
- After filling up my tumbler, I will put on my favorite podcast while I prepare for the day.

Evening routine:

- After dinner, I will read at least one page of a book to my kids.
- After putting my kids to bed, I will write at least one sentence about my day in my journal.
- After writing down something about my day, I will write down something I'm grateful for and three wins I've had during the day.
- After writing down my gratitude and wins, I will read something I enjoy for at least five minutes.
- Before I go to sleep, I will take out my workout clothes for the next day.

See how, in each of these examples, there are clear cues to where each part of the routine starts. There are no questions about what is supposed to be done or when. It's also straightforward to complete. Both routines could be finished in under 10 minutes total, if necessary. But the chances are, as they start, they will gain momentum and go even longer.

There's no right or wrong regarding what to include in your morning routine. You'll want to use your discoveries from this book so far and your goals and intentions set with your vision board to choose what will work best for your morning and evening routine.

By creating and sticking to a morning routine, you are showing a commitment to yourself by making time for those things that are important to you. You're creating an identity that you are a person who does these things, no matter what.

Creating & Honoring Boundaries

Our initial "quick wins" at the beginning of this chapter empowered us to gain clarity on our desires so we can take purposeful actions. Another crucial aspect of aligning ourselves involves deciding what we want rather than letting external circumstances dictate our path.

Consider Paula, a dedicated kindergarten teacher at a prestigious private school. Despite her passion for teaching, she feels overwhelmed by the constant demand for her attention. Emails from parents and colleagues flood her inbox 24/7. Each email sends a new notification to her phone, and she is urged to respond immediately. And now that she's been reacting quickly, the parents seem to anticipate quick responses.

Adding to the strain, Paula takes her daughter to her competitive gymnastics practice every day after school. Without fail, one of the moms likes to talk to her about an upcoming election and her strong political views. Paula isn't comfortable with this topic of discussion and tries to change the subject, but usually without success. She nods and agrees with statements that she doesn't believe to avoid conflict, making her feel inauthentic.

Between the emails and political discussions, Paula finds herself physically and mentally exhausted at the end of the day. She has no energy left for what she truly wants to do for herself: writing the fantasy novel she'd dreamed of writing since she was a little girl.

Paula could benefit from establishing clear boundaries to reclaim her time and mental space. Let's talk about what a boundary is. A boundary is not something we use to control other people. It is something that *we* choose to do when a limit we have decided on has been crossed. For example, you might have a boundary that you will leave the room if someone yells at you. The boundary isn't "you can't yell at me;" it's "if you yell at me, I will leave the room." The boundary is what *you* will do if they choose to take that action.

If you are feeling angry at the person you want to create a boundary with, it's not time to communicate the boundary quite yet. You will want to process your emotions and regulate yourself first to hold the boundary from a clean space. You can choose any exercise from Chapters Four or Five to do this, such as taking some slow, light, and deep breaths or naming the emotion and doing a body scan.

Setting boundaries isn't about manipulating other people but honoring ourselves. You can feel peaceful and even loving while setting a boundary. They often allow you to feel more love for the other person. You won't be feeling resentment because you have that healthy boundary.

Boundaries can be set to safeguard various aspects, such as to protect our time, our emotions, our bodies, and our mental well-being. In Paula's case, boundaries around her time (regarding school emails) and her mental space (regarding political conversations) could significantly enhance her well-being.

Notice that Paula thinks that she's on call all the time whenever parents email her, but she doesn't have to be. She could turn the notifications off on her phone and tell her parents and coworkers that she won't respond to emails after hours. Similarly, when faced with uncomfortable political discussions, a simple declaration like, "I'm not comfortable discussing politics; let's talk about something else, or I'll need to step away," can be empowering.

These boundaries could save Paula time and mental space that she could use towards creating the life she wants. It's important to remember that our boundaries only work as well as we honor them. Once we set a boundary, we need to do what we say we will do. For example, if Paula says she isn't going to respond to emails after hours, but she does it anyway, then the parents will continue to expect her to respond to emails.

We can work on having our own back with those boundaries. The more we practice this self-advocacy, the more adept we become at preserving our time, energy, and space. Remember, what other people think about our choices is *their* business, not ours. What other people think about us is none of our business.

Boundaries are a powerful tool for creating the conditions to shape the lives we aspire to lead. In your free workbook (www.teachergoals.com/educate-resources), you'll find a boundaries chart where you can define your boundaries and what you will do if a boundary is crossed.

As you apply the tools you've learned in this chapter, such as setting boundaries, creating a vision board, and creating habits through a morning and evening routine, you'll find yourself getting more aligned with what you truly desire in teaching and life. You'll be ready to soar to even greater heights!

10

Intentional Scheduling

"I planned to go to the gym after school…but then I found myself helping a coworker who needed help. The next thing I knew, we were chatting about the latest episode of "The Real Housewives," and I realized it was an hour past when I planned on leaving. I had to hurry and pick up the kids from daycare and get dinner on the table. I'm such a mess!" Lisa groaned as the waitress walked away, leaving us with our unlimited soup, salad, and breadsticks.

"You're not a mess!" I assured her, as I tossed the salad. "As one of my favorite authors Kristina Kuzmic says, it is essential to 'give yourself more compassion than criticism, more grace than judgment (Kuzmic, 2020).'"

"You're a life coach, can you help me figure out what's going on?" she asked. Of course, I was happy to help her. In between bites, we discussed what it was that stopped her from making it to the gym. She had a big heart and wanted to help her coworkers, and she loved to chat and connect with others. There is nothing wrong with either of those things: these show what she values.

At the same time, going to the gym was her goal and something she wanted to do. She had the big picture and her "why." But how could she ensure that those things happen instead of repeating the same scenario day after day when new fires arise?

This is where we looked at creating an intentional schedule that works for Lisa. How could we ensure there was some space to help and connect with coworkers while allowing her to get to the gym before getting dinner for her family?

We observed her plan to go to the gym to see if it was a time problem or a boundary problem. It looked like it was a case of both—since she said "yes" to helping her coworker when she'd made plans with herself, but she also squeezed the gym into a time frame with an expectation that may not have been ideal for her schedule, either. Then, we ensured she planned her gym time into an intentional schedule.

"Don't forget that one setback doesn't deter us from getting where we want to go," I assured Lisa. "It's all about noticing what didn't go right and reflecting on what we can do better the next day."

"I feel so much better now just talking it out!" said Lisa, as she grabbed the check. "I think this calls for a celebration! Let's go get a pedicure."

Chances are, you run into similar situations in your day-to-day life. So far in these pages, we've been diving into your desires, choosing the direction you want to go, setting goals, and creating an overall vision for your life. Now, it's time to put it into action daily, where new opportunities to choose your path arrive each day. That is where intentional planning and scheduling come in, as well as consistent reflection and grace as we go.

The Urgency Effect

"I have two kinds of problems, the urgent and the important. The urgent are not important, and the important are never urgent." This relatable quote came from none other than Dwight D. Eisenhower in a 1954 speech (Eisenhower, 1954). As the 34th president of the United States, we can easily assume that he knew a thing or two about urgent tasks.

This isn't all he had to say about the matter. He is also credited with saying, "Who can define the difference between the long and short term for us with accuracy! Especially whenever our affairs seem to be in crisis, we are almost compelled to give our first attention to the urgent present rather than to the important future."

How often do you find yourself suddenly in a moment of crisis as an educator? Whether you're teaching a class of 30 kids, homeschooling your children at your kitchen table, or an administrator running a Title One school, chances are, these mini crises happen frequently.

Maybe a child has a meltdown, or you realize that you forgot to make the copies you needed for one of your lessons, or you have an upset parent. Situations like this come up that need to be addressed at the moment. However, a week or a month from now, that one problem might not matter.

The problem comes when these urgent tasks add up to the point where they prevent us from completing important tasks that may matter even more in the long term but don't need to be completed in the short term. When we fill our schedule to the max, we don't allow time for situations like this, and essential tasks keep getting pushed back. Sometimes, they get pushed back to the point that they just don't happen. This is called the "urgency effect." Often, the result of this is that we feel burned out from doing so much, yet unfulfilled because we don't make the time for what's most aligned to our core values.

Stephen Covey, author of *The Seven Habits of Highly Effective People,* sought a solution to this problem. He took this urgent versus important concept from Eisenhower and turned it into the Eisenhower Matrix chart, as seen below (Covey, 2004). Tasks are divided into one of four categories, and each category has a suggestion for what to do with each type of task:

- ***Urgent & Important:*** Do it right away or schedule it very soon.
- ***Not Urgent & Important:*** Schedule a time to ensure it happens so it doesn't get lost in the sea of "urgent and not important" tasks.
- ***Urgent & Not Important:*** See if you can delegate whenever possible (online grocery pickup/delivery, parent/kid helpers, etc.). When you can't delegate a task, consider what you *can* delegate to create more time and mental space for what you need to do. For example, you can delegate your grocery shopping by having Instacart bring you groceries to save yourself time, or some of your planning by getting a resource from Teachers pay Teachers)
- ***Not Urgent & Not Important:*** Ask, *"Does this need to be done?"* Consider simplifying and removing this task. For example, you may not need to grade every single assignment your students complete.

Figure 10.1
Urgency Matrix

This matrix can be handy as we plan our weeks to ensure a well-balanced schedule of all of your tasks.

For example, the "urgency effect" situation arose while writing this book. Getting this book into the world is my most important project of the entire year. Still, as I got to work each day, more urgent tasks would arise, such as recording an episode for the next week of the podcast, answering questions for my team, and driving my daughter, Brielle, around to her various music and theatre practices. These things needed to be done sooner than my next book deadline, but I noticed the culmination of these "urgent" tasks prevented me from making the needed progress on this book, which was more "important" long-term.

After noticing the urgency effect in action, I had to adjust. So, I looked at my tasks and considered where they fit in the urgency matrix. I had to look at what was taking up my time that felt "urgent" but not "important."

I realized that the podcast had been "urgent" each week, and while the podcast is important to me, each individual episode wasn't as crucial as completing my book and bringing it to life. I also realized that getting too involved in my team's tasks wasn't giving me enough time to complete my own. Finally, I realized I could work with my husband (a work-from-home parent like myself) to create a different homeschool schedule for a season while completing the book.

To accomplish this, I had several periods where we ran "replay" episodes on the podcast. I would record just a short insight before playing a previous episode or share a clip from an earlier Educate & Rejuvenate session or a coaching call from our membership. While I ideally like to release brand new content every week, this solution gave me the time I needed to complete this book while keeping my commitment to releasing something to the podcast feed each week.

I also discussed problem-solving strategies with my team and trusted them to make decisions. Additionally, I planned blocks of time in advance to support them in their tasks, preventing last-minute surprises that could disrupt my schedule. And lastly, my husband and I adjusted our homeschool schedule to allow me to have more time in the mornings to work on my book.

Suddenly, I had way more time, energy, and mental space to devote to pouring my heart and soul into the pages you are reading. This is the power of the urgency matrix. We will utilize this matrix to create our ideal week and weekly planning.

Create Your Ideal Week

Planning can feel daunting when starting with a blank slate. But what if you didn't have to? Creating an ideal week involves creating a basic schedule template for what you want your days to look like so you don't have to start from scratch with your planning.

To complete this exercise, you must first list all the scheduled things that happen each week. I've included a blank template in your free workbook to simplify this exercise. Here is a list of things you might have to add to your ideal week:

- Contract hours or current homeschool schedule for homeschool parents
- You can decide whether to include your school schedule in more detail in your ideal week or, if you have that in your teacher planner, block off those hours as "teaching."
- Weekly meetings, committees, co-ops, after-school activities, or any other "extras" in your teaching schedule
- Weekly classes, lessons, or activities for yourself
- Weekly classes, lessons, or activities for anyone else in your family
- Regularly scheduled volunteer work or side hustle work time
- Church or worship services, if applicable

Next, you'll want to list everything you want to complete for self-care each week.

- Your morning/evening routine
- Time for exercise/moving your body
- Time for enough sleep
- Time for hobbies and things you love
- White space in your calendar to give yourself some space as well as time for when the unexpected happens

Finally, list all the things that tend to find their way into your schedule unexpectedly, such as time to help or chat with coworkers or unstructured family time, and schedule it into your ideal week. When you finish your ideal week, it might look something like this:

Figure 10.2
Ideal Week Example

	Monday	Tuesday	Wednesday	Thursday	Friday	Saturday	Sunday
5 AM - 6 AM							
6 AM - 7 AM	Go in early to plan	Yoga Class	Staff Mtg	Yoga Class	Work on side hustle		SLEEP IN!
7 AM - 8 AM							
8 AM - 9 AM	Teach	Teach				High Fitness	
9 AM - 10 AM							Family Worship/
10 AM - 11 AM							Outside Time
11 AM - 12 PM							
12 PM - 1 PM							
1 PM - 2 PM						Kids Soccer	
2 PM - 3 PM					PLCs		
3 PM - 4 PM							
4 PM - 5 PM		Committee Meeting					
5 PM - 6 PM	Piano Lessons				Fam Movie Night &		
6 PM - 7 PM		Gymnastics		Soccer Practices	Pizza Night		Dinner
7 PM - 8 PM							Plan next week
8 PM - 9 PM	Bedtime w/ Kids						
9 PM - 10 PM	Me Time		Work on side hustle				
10 PM - 11 PM	My Bedtime						

This will give you a great template to start as you plan each week. It doesn't mean you will stick to it precisely every week. You'll need to adjust your calendar as one-time events arise. However, having an "ideal week" in mind helps you have a framework, making weekly planning much more manageable. Instead of staring at a blank page, ask yourself, *"What do I need to adjust this week?"*

Weekly Schedule Planning

Once you've created your ideal week, your weekly schedule planning is already off to a great start! Now, it's time to tweak and customize it based on your workload and personal needs each week. Taking one hour to plan your week intentionally will make the rest of the week flow more easily. This is separate from your lesson planning. However, you could piggy-back your overall weekly planning with your weekly lesson planning.

To start, you'll want to decide when you'll do your weekly planning. Will you do it on Friday before heading off for the weekend? Sunday night? Early Monday morning? It doesn't matter exactly when it is; just that you find a consistent time that works for you. Once you get used to this system, it will likely take less than an hour, especially with your ideal week as a starting point.

To start each week of planning, make a list of all of your to-dos for the week. It's just like a brain dump or thought download about your thoughts, but for all of your to-dos this week. Don't self-edit yet—just let your pen flow with everything your brain tells you to do this week.

I love this exercise because we often tell ourselves, *"I'm so busy!"* and *"I have so much to do!"* By writing it all down, we can neutralize it by getting to the facts of the situation. Oftentimes, each task doesn't necessarily take us as long as we are making it out to be, and each task might not even be as important or necessary as our subconscious brains are telling us they are. Once you've completed the exercise, you'll have a physical piece of paper with all of those things outside of you, so your mind no longer needs to keep track of everything. And you'll now be able to look at that list more objectively.

Next, you'll analyze the list of tasks and prioritize them, keeping the "urgency matrix" in mind. Make sure any "urgent and important" tasks fit first, then make room for the "important but not as urgent" ones. And, most importantly, question everything on your list and ask yourself, *"Does this need to be done, and if so, does it need to be done by me?"* This is where you tap into the alignment we've been discussing, ensuring the tasks you put on your list are the most important to you. Ask yourself, *"What can you eliminate or delegate this week?"*

Then, using the ideal week you created as a starting point, plug in your scheduled responsibilities (contract hours, teaching, prep periods, appointments, kids' activities, etc.) and the self-care blocks you created in your ideal week into your schedule. If you need to adjust the ideal week schedule (say, to make room for a one-time appointment) then make sure you move the self-care somewhere else, so it still happens.

Then, we get out your task list and start breaking it down by day first. Make a list of each day like this:

Monday:

Tuesday:

Wednesday:

Thursday:

Friday:

Saturday:

Sunday:

There may be some shuffling around as you plan to ensure the tasks have enough room to fit each day as you look at your calendar so far. Once you've finalized your list and it is good to go, you will plug each to-do into a time slot in your calendar. Make sure to give yourself *more* time than you think you will need for each task and to leave some white space in your calendar.

Once your calendar is complete, you are no longer working off a running to-do list (that you'll have to keep thinking about in your head). Now, you have it all down in your calendar so that you can pull out your calendar each day and see your to-dos. Your mind can rest easily.

There is a chance your brain is fighting back on me with this scheduling. You might think, *"There is no way this will work FOR ME!"* or *"Writing down EVERYTHING I need to do will make me feel more overwhelmed."* Our subconscious brain doesn't like change, so it'll prefer to do what you're currently doing since it's more comfortable. All I ask is that you give it a try for a few weeks. Chances are, you'll find a flow that works perfectly, even if it's slightly different from how I've outlined it here.

As you go through your week, things that impact your schedule will come up. We aren't robots and will need to adjust our schedule at times. We must leave more time than necessary for each task and leave some white space in our calendar so you can move things somewhere else if things come up.

Reflecting on How the Week Went

At the end of the week, it is time to reflect on how the week went. This is where we ask ourselves how well we stuck to our plan for the week and if everything important was done. If yes, amazing! If not, that's okay—we can look at what wins we had throughout the week, assess what didn't go quite right, and learn from the information we observe.

The good news is the reason it didn't work will likely fit into one of these patterns listed below. Consider which of the following reasons might have impacted your schedule for the week. Each one has a solution you can try moving forward.

These are some of the most common reasons we sometimes don't stick to our schedules:

Lack of Boundaries

As educators, we have big hearts. It comes with the profession, as those who love to help others are drawn to education. However, sometimes, we do this to a fault by putting other people's priorities above our own—and this is when a lack of boundaries can become an issue when we are trying to stick to a schedule.

Lisa's example at the beginning of the chapter was an example of a boundary issue. She wanted to go to the gym after school, but when her coworker needed help, her plans went out the window.

Instead, we can treat the time we have planned for specific tasks (prep time, gym time, or time spent working towards a goal) just like a dentist appointment that must be rescheduled. If there is nowhere to move it, you can just let the other person know that you can't do it at that time and that you'll be happy to help them another time. Michelle Obama once said, "We need to do a better job putting ourselves higher on our own to-do list (Obama, 2016)." Holding boundaries allows us to honor the commitments we've made to ourselves.

Trying to Fit Too Many Things in Too Small of a Time Frame

Lisa's example at the beginning of the chapter also had this issue. Not only did she spend time chatting with her coworker, but she realized that the time frame she had for the gym ended up not feeling realistic in the time frame she put it in. Maybe she wants to be able to help her coworkers after school and go to the gym. In that case, she needs to make a different plan.

When we pile too many things into one window, we might feel like failures when we don't complete them all when what we asked of ourselves was impossible. After all, we are human and have the same 24 hours daily. If you find this happening too often, you need to simplify. Try to think outside the box and see what you can do.

Not Having Open Space to Rearrange the Schedule as Needed

Like the last point, if we put too much into too little of a time period consistently throughout the week, then there is no white space to adjust our schedule as needed.

Not Following Through for Other Reasons: How Were We Feeling? What Was Our Mindset?

Sometimes we don't do anything because we are dysregulated or avoiding or resisting emotions. We may also be thinking thoughts that are disempowering ourselves. Take a moment to observe yourself and see if you need to utilize any of the tools at the beginning of this book

Seasons Change

What works for one season may not work for another. If you find a schedule that used to work consistently not working, it's time to ask if there's been a change in the season of your life that means you need to change.

The Unexpected Happened

Two weeks ago, I had a whole week planned ahead, which I was eager and excited about. I had some exciting homeschool lessons for my kids using the engaging children's book *Peter O'Meter* by Tricia Fuglestad. I was continuing to plug away and make progress on writing this book, and some exciting coaching workshops were happening. My week was off to a great start as I woke up on time and was just about to finish stretching from my workout when the phone rang. It was my dad. My grandpa had just died.

I knew I needed to lighten my load that week versus what I had planned. So, what did I do (after wiping my tears and processing the shock)? I reassessed my calendar and only completed tasks that week that were both "urgent" and "important," meaning the main tasks I did for work that week were showing up to teach the vision board challenge and answering urgent questions from my team. Other than that, I moved whatever I could to the next week so I could give myself space to move through the emotions of grief. I wouldn't have been able to do that had I not already had a prioritized to do list, so little did I know how much this pre-planning made this difficult moment easier to manage.

Sometimes, things come up during our week that we couldn't have imagined. When this happens, you can reassess at any time. As we've learned in this book, taking care of ourselves is the most important. Sometimes, that means we need to step back rather than push through. Sometimes, incredible opportunities make it worth pushing back some things occasionally.

Other times, we can't fully adjust our schedule, but we can take moments to process our emotions and regulate our nervous system. If every week starts to feel like this, though, then that means it may be time to reassess your schedule as a whole.

Having Self-Compassion if Things Didn't Go 100% as Planned

If everything doesn't go exactly how you planned, you can show yourself compassion. No matter the reason, you can learn the lessons and forgive yourself quickly. The most critical part of progressing towards what you want is how YOU treat yourself.

To gain a deeper understanding of how you spend your time, consider doing a time audit. Keep a notebook or use a notes app for an entire week, and record everything you do in 15-minute increments. While this may be challenging during the school day, just do your best. We also have a time audit exercise inside the PDF workbook. This exercise will give you a lot of awareness about how you spend your time and help you adjust going forward.

While you're reflecting on your week, it's not just about if you completed everything but also how you treated yourself. Did you stick to your schedule, but you overpacked it so much that you are exhausted? Is it sustainable in the long term? Did you make enough time for the things you love? Your weekly reflection is a great time to circle back to the self-coaching tools we have been teaching throughout the book. Try doing a thought download about your week to understand how it went more holistically.

Whenever a day or week doesn't go as planned, and essential things on your list don't get done, give yourself grace and ask yourself how you were feeling and what you were thinking throughout the week. Look at what went right to keep doing what was working. As we practice creating and sticking to an intentional schedule, we learn what works and what doesn't and make incremental improvements over time.

Once you get into your groove, you'll find that your days flow more smoothly, your productivity increases, and your overall sense of well-being improves. So, embrace the journey, knowing that each step forward, no matter how small, brings you closer to being more aligned in teaching and in life.

11

Embracing the Educate & Rejuvenate Journey

While mindlessly scrolling social media, I saw a video that took my breath away: a simple yet profound acrobatic routine utilizing a trampoline and a staircase. French dancer and choreographer Yoann Bourgeois created a routine that was a metaphor for life (Now This Impact, 2022). He was walking up a flight of stairs, free-falling, landing on the trampoline, and bouncing back up again. Sometimes, he'd land a step ahead of where he was. Other times, he'd land three steps back. He'd almost approach the top of the staircase, arms outstretched to something just out of reach… and fall. At one point, he reached the top but looked down and fell out of fear. He'd get back up and fall again…and again and again.

This video is a metaphor for life, and it was an essential reminder of the experience I've had the last few years of my life. I saw massive success over the first five years when I started my company as "Wife Teacher Mommy" on Teachers Pay Teachers (TPT) before our recent rebrand to Educate & Rejuvenate. I brought my husband home to help me with the kids and running the company and expanded to hire incredible team members to help me.

And then, there was a perfect storm. First, the school closures of the pandemic made our sub plans (our main source of sales) irrelevant. We quickly pivoted to online resources and home learning packets, and they soared...temporarily. We made decisions going forward based on the trends we'd been seeing. While our expenses skyrocketed through our investments, sales started plummeting again due to the changing education landscape, TPT marketplace & social media algorithm changes, and so much more.

Suddenly, I didn't feel like a success anymore, but I felt the weight of my family and employees depending on me. I didn't understand why this would happen after I'd found life coaching, and I'd been doing more mindset work than ever. I was shifting my thoughts, processing my emotions, and regulating myself whenever possible. How could I be doing everything right, but everything was going wrong?

As I watched this video, I suddenly saw myself as the acrobat on the staircase, plummeting from the tops of success back to the bottom and continuing to bounce back even among the setbacks. And I knew that was what I had to do, and what I'm still doing.

The struggles I've faced in my business are precisely how it was supposed to happen. If it hadn't, I would have stayed in my comfort zone. I'd still only be making printables. I never would have thought of starting a membership, hosting a virtual conference, and bringing thousands of educators together live. I probably would have kept telling myself, "I don't have time" to certify as a life coach, even though it had become my dream. And that means that you wouldn't be reading this book, either.

I've stepped out of my comfort zone and faced each setback with grit, knowing that I will bounce back even as I keep falling sometimes when it seems like everything going wrong is taking us where we are meant to go.

I share this story because I want to be honest with you. You will continue to face obstacles and roadblocks as you apply this framework to your life. You must be resilient to keep going when things aren't going exactly how you want them to. I don't want you to give up at the first setback as you start putting what you've learned from this book into action.

You might be buzzing with ideas and inspiration as you read this book. You might tell yourself, "It's only going to go up from here!" We tend to feel empowered when reading a personal development book like this, attending a professional development conference, or attending a webinar.

But, like in the staircase video, what goes up must also come down. And then, as soon as we have a setback, we question ourselves. You might go from that extreme "high" back to an even lower "low" because you got a taste of what was possible, but then think that it's not possible for you because you "messed up" or things aren't going exactly the way you imagined.

You may notice your inner critic creeping up even after implementing these tools. You might start using the self-coaching model to beat yourself up, berating yourself for not thinking differently. Or perhaps you won't notice yourself resisting emotions until you take out your anger in class. You might believe the tools work in theory, but you think they don't work for you because something is wrong with you.

The truth is the exact opposite. Everything is happening as it needs to for your benefit. Part of the process is realizing and understanding that growth is not linear. As we learn and apply these tools, our brain tends to serve us all the thoughts about the things that go wrong every day. This is because, as discussed in previous chapters, our brains are wired to protect us and subconsciously look for the negative.

Of course, it will take time to rewire our thinking patterns and learn how to create new habits. After all, we've spent years building our current belief systems and processes. You won't finish this book and suddenly have unraveled all of it. And that's not even the point. We are human and always will be, flaws and all.

We can see our lives the same way we do our lesson plans. While we make a plan, we still have to adjust it, pivot, and redirect as needed. As spiritual teacher Gabrielle Bernstein says, "Obstacles are detours in the right direction (Bernstein, 2016)." Every setback can help you get closer to where you are meant to be. This is all part of the process; we don't need to fear falling. As Martin Luther King, Jr. once said, "Faith is taking the first step, even when you don't see the whole staircase (Nysmuseum, 2014)." We may not know when we'll make it to the top of the staircase or how often we'll fall on the trampoline, but we can still believe in ourselves and our ability to bounce back.

Improving Your Comeback Rate

Our success is not dependent on us always thinking the right thoughts or feeling happy 100% of the time. We must believe we can catch ourselves faster each time and choose again. Gabrielle Bernstein explains, "A quick comeback rate is how quickly you restore your thoughts to love (Klug & Bernstein, 2016)." Simply put, we increase our comeback rate as we get faster at noticing when we have a negative thought or feeling and redirecting.

You should celebrate each time you catch yourself and choose again because that means you are becoming self-aware and have the opportunity to practice catching yourself and redirecting. Before reading this book, you may have never noticed, and your subconscious might have kept in control. Now, you can do something about it, and each time you do, you're flexing the muscles and creating new neuropathways that will make it easier next time.

Let's take buffering (avoiding emotions) with food as an example of how you'll see improvements. Let's say you have a problem with going to the pantry and binge eating whenever you feel stressed when you get home from school. When you're first applying this work, you might not notice until after you've eaten an entire sleeve of Oreos. But you still noticed and were able to identify that you were resisting your emotions. This is an improvement because you gained awareness!

Then, the next time, maybe you'll notice after you eat just one Oreo. Later, you might see yourself as you're walking to the pantry and realize, "Wait a minute! I'm not hungry. This is just stress." Eventually, you might even notice the subconscious alarm bell thought, "This is too stressful!" come up before you make it to the pantry. Instead, you'll process your emotions or shift your thoughts. As you can see, we can improve where we catch ourselves, choose again, and align ourselves.

Instead of being hung up on instant improvement, believe you are making progress, even if it looks different than you imagined. Embrace the journey because you're exactly where you need to be. Ask yourself, *"How can I enjoy this process even more? How can I make reaching my goals and my dream life more fun?"*

This work aims to continue following these three steps every day. We will get even better at observing ourselves more naturally, making it easier to continue choosing our direction and aligning ourselves with it.

Reassess Your Direction as Needed

The central part of aligning ourselves that we've been discussing so far is ensuring we are headed in the chosen direction.

But does this mean we can't change course once we've selected our direction? One important part of "aligning ourselves" is assessing if our direction is where we want to go.

For example, I was coaching someone (we'll call him David) who thought he wanted to go the administrator route with his career. He had set some big goals, enrolled in courses, and started looking into how to uplevel his career. However, at the same time, he wanted to have more time for his family. He realized he didn't want to go on that track in his career at the current phase of his life. He still wanted to do it at some point but hit the "pause" button for the moment.

Does this mean he "gave up?" Not at all! Sometimes, we choose a direction that isn't in alignment with our values. We might set a goal or choose a direction with good intentions but realize it isn't where we want to go. It is a huge win when we recognize this because we are getting to know our authentic selves and true desires even more. We may have never known it wasn't what we wanted until we started going that route. Whether we end up there or change course before we get there, we can see that we are going exactly where we need to be, as long as we come about it with a clear mind and heart rather than fear or scarcity.

Focusing on One Percent Improvement

What if you only tried to improve by one percent each day instead of growing by leaps and bounds overnight? Sometimes, we want to grow exponentially, but slow and steady wins the race, just like we may teach our kids in Aesop's fable "The Tortoise and the Hare."

Author James Clear shares how the math of one percent improvement shows up over one year in his book *Atomic Habits*:

"If you can get 1% better each day for one year, you'll end up thirty-seven times better by the time you're done. Conversely, if you get 1% worse each day for one year, you'll decline nearly down to zero. What starts as a small win or a minor setback accumulates into something much more (Clear, 2018)."

This concept is called the "aggregation of marginal gains," a term penned by British cycling performance director Dave Brailsford, who led his team from mediocre (at best) to seemingly overnight success by focusing on one percent improvements in every area possible—from improving bike grips, encouraging his team to wash their hands to stay healthy, to getting the best mattresses they could find for better sleep. These tiny measurements added up, and their league won countless victories by focusing on improving by one percent.

One percent improvement might not be meaningful alone or even noticed in your daily life. But as we improve, little by little, we will see a difference. All you need to do is focus on just one small thing each day that your future self will thank you for.

Even if these incremental changes don't seem noticeable initially, keeping track of your improvements can help you see them over time. This will help you see your forward motion towards your goal. You can keep track of your progress in a journal, using an app (such as Streaks or Habitica for habit tracking), or even a simple spreadsheet. We've also included a habit tracker inside your Educate & Rejuvenate PDF workbook. Whatever you decide to do, make sure you have some way of actually seeing and noticing the progress. One percent improvements might feel small, but if you pay attention over time, you'll see them add up!

Owning Our Wins Along The Way

When I started working with my first life coach, Lizzie, we had a 45-minute weekly virtual session. Working one-on-one with a life coach was a huge investment for me; over the first year of working with a coach, I spent thousands of dollars, and that was not a small amount for our average middle-class family, but it was well worth every penny. However, I initially felt annoyed when we started each call with "celebrations." I thought, *"I'm paying good money for these calls. We need to get right into solving my problems, not spend five minutes talking about my wins!"*

Hilariously, I was thinking this as someone who already knew and understood that my thoughts create my feelings and invested a ton of money to work with a coach on my mindset, so it was ironic that my mindset about looking at the wins was so negative. I didn't realize the importance of this part of our calls and how it helped me frame my mindset before diving into what I would consider my problems. Over time, I started to get grateful that we began our sessions with this, but it shows that so many of us naturally think it is a waste of time to look at our wins. We believe we have too much to do, too many other things to worry about, that maybe I'll do that at some point, but I don't have time to own my wins.

Just like all the tools in this book, it doesn't take much time to look at your wins, but it makes a massive difference in your thoughts, feelings, and actions in your day-to-day life. If we only took a few minutes each day to do this, or reframe our thoughts to look for a win when a negative thought comes up, we'd feel a lot better! Let's look at how this helped one of the educators in our community.

Katie's Story of Owning Her Wins & Tracking Progress

Years after my own realization with my life coach, I've seen other educators come to the same realization. Let's take Katie, an educator from our Educate & Rejuvenate Club community, as an example. She was an English and theatre teacher at a middle school. As the school year was ending and the kids were cleaning out their lockers, she explained on one of our community coaching calls that she felt that even though she had accomplished some things, it wasn't enough and didn't *feel* accomplished.

As her life coach, I immediately wondered what she was thinking that made her feel unaccomplished. So I asked her, "Why do you think you don't feel accomplished?"

She said, "Well, I am working as a provisional teacher while I complete my teaching licensure. I stayed at home with my kids for the past 15 years, so teaching in a classroom is new. I feel like I'm flying by the seat of my pants! I'm getting great marks on my observations, but I just thought I would feel more accomplished by now!"

We discussed that her lack of feeling accomplished had nothing to do with what she had or hadn't done (remember, actions we have taken in the past are now a circumstance). Instead, it was the way she was thinking about it.

"I think that the thoughts you're telling yourself about not knowing what you're doing seem to be a sticking point for you. That, and possibly what you're making being a provisional teacher mean, since that's what you brought up first. Would you agree?"

She agreed. I followed up with, "What if there's nothing wrong with making it up as you go? Kids need us to adjust our plans to meet their needs, and if we're too set in what we're going to do, we can't do that."

She nodded and found this interesting. Additionally, I pointed Katie towards the comments in the webinar chat that other educators in our community were sharing. They shared things such as "I've been teaching for 18 years, and I still fly by the seat of my pants!" and "You're in good company."

I pointed out that thinking that you're flying by the seat of your pants and going with the flow isn't always a problem. What matters is what we make it mean. Some teachers may say, "Oh, I make it up as I go, and somehow it all works out," and they feel confident, while others think it's a problem because they think it means something inadequate about them. So, likely, there's something even more profound than just "I don't know what I'm doing." I asked Katie what she thought that might be.

She said, "I think what I'm thinking is that I'm just not enough." She explained that she felt very insecure as a teacher and always second-guessed everything she did. If she was thinking *"I'm not enough,"* no wonder she wasn't feeling accomplished!

I asked her why she felt like she wasn't enough. She said she compared herself to all the other teachers in her building, who had much more organized classrooms.

I told her those teachers have their strengths, but so did she. What were some of hers?

She thought for a second and then said, "Well, I guess I was the only teacher in the building who directed not one but two school plays this year! And the kids always like to come hang out in the theater room after school. I've cultivated a safe space for the theater kids! I guess that counts for something." Her eyebrows lifted as her face brightened into a smile, and she stifled a laugh. Then she added, "Wow, you know what? Now I feel accomplished!"

I congratulated her for taking the time to reframe her thoughts and look at her wins. Then, I taught her the skill I mentioned in this book, "The Gap and The Gain," and how I recommend journaling about your wins. In case you forgot from the previous chapters, this is the concept by Dan Sullivan where we want to compare ourselves to how far we've come and use that momentum to propel ourselves forward instead of constantly comparing ourselves to an ever-moving goalpost and feeling like we aren't enough (Sullivan & Hardy, 2021).

The journal process I recommended to keep Katie in "The Gain" is one you can utilize, too. Here is the process:

- Start in the evening on Day One and write three wins you had that day in your journal.
- Then, after you write your wins, you'll write three that you plan to have the next day. Stick to only three and make them specific.
- Then, the next day, you'll get out your journal and review the wins you wrote the previous day, write your three wins for the day, and write what three wins you'll have the next day.

What usually happens after following this process is that you'll open up your journal to write your wins for the day, and you'll be able to say, *"Yes, I did those things I said I would do. Wow, I really do keep my promises to myself!"* You'll be able to step into that identity of someone who does what they say they are going to do!

Compare this to if you wrote down a list of 20 to-dos and only completed six. You might feel defeated. But if you list three and then you do six, you completed double what you said you would do. It's the same thing, but a different mindset that will set you up for success. You will then repeat this cycle daily. After a week, you'll be amazed to see how much you've accomplished! Every little bit adds up.

Looking at our wins matters because how we look at the past frames our future. What we think about is in the past; it's already happened. Like our selective attention, our selective memory remembers what proves our thinking right. This is why two people can give very different testimonies to something that happened, even though they were both there.

If you're looking at your week and thinking about how much you haven't done and that means there's no way that you can do everyting you want, you're right, because that's the energy you'll bring into your future. Instead, we can train our brains by taking the time to consciously look at our wins and lessons learned from losses and accept that our past is just what we need to grow and get to where we are right now.

Take a moment right now to consider three wins you've had today. For one, you are almost finished with this book and have learned many tools to help you create the life you want! The future is bright, and yours for the taking when you take control of who you want to be.

Educating & Rejuvenating Together

Sometimes, you can find inspiration where you least expect it. I didn't expect to find an incredible coaching moment from a fictional soccer coach on a comedy TV show called "Ted Lasso." I had zero interest in this show (as I'm not into sports), but my husband convinced me to try it, and now it's one of my favorite TV shows. While Ted Lasso was a sports coach, he also regularly showed himself as a life coach for his team and colleagues (Hunt et al., 2020).

One of my favorite scenes in the show is when Ted Lasso gives his team a pep talk after they've lost a crucial game. He reminds them that they played a good match even though they didn't win. He names some of his team members' independent wins (just like we, as educators, love to do with our students) to lift their spirits while admitting that it's a sad moment. But Ted urges them to look around the locker room and see they aren't alone. He says, "There's something worse than being sad, and that's being alone and being sad. No one in this room is alone."

As educators, we also face struggles, wins, and losses. There will be times when we feel sad, angry, or stressed. But we don't have to go about teaching alone. Combining the tools and concepts from this book with community and connection makes it even more powerful...and the numbers backing this statement don't lie!

A groundbreaking study involving over 1000 women physician trainees across 26 medical institutions revealed significant improvements in well-being through a four-month online group coaching program. Participants reported experiencing less emotional exhaustion, a sense of disconnect from themselves (depersonalization), feeling like they're not as competent as others perceive them to be (imposter syndrome), and distress caused by actions conflicting with their moral values (moral injury). They also showed increased self-compassion, as measured by the Neff Self-Compassion Scale-Short Form, and improved overall flourishing according to the standardized Secure Flourish Index. These findings highlight the transformative potential of using coaching tools within a group setting to foster connection and alleviate professional distress (Mann et al., 2023).

While I don't have quantitative data on how our group coaching has impacted educators just yet, we can safely assume that these findings would translate to our field as well, as the self-coaching model used in the study is the same one I taught in this book and that we utilize in our coaching. Additionally, the qualitative data we've seen in the past two years of offering coaching has showed a significant impact on those who have participated.

One of our Educate & Rejuvenate members said that her favorite part of the coaching is how the community comes together. When she hears the problems others are facing, she realizes that she often has the same things going on, even if they present themselves differently. In this safe space, we learn from each other and how to shift our mindset and strategize together.

Whenever an educator comes on camera to be coached and opens up about their real struggles with vulnerability, they spread love to all those who hear and can relate to their story and struggles. That love is reflected right back to them in comments like these:

Figure 11.1
Love and Support from Educators

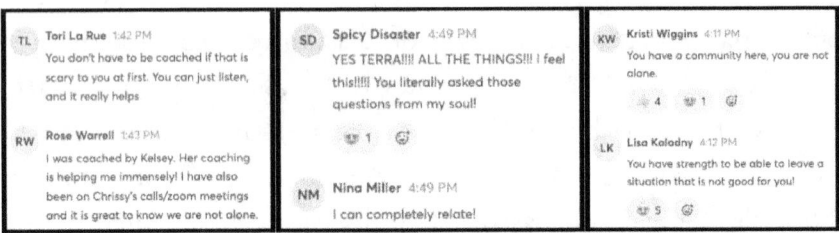

Sharing our struggles in a safe space fosters the sense of love and belonging we all seek. Instead of feeling like we need to please others or be anything other than who we are, we are celebrated for being our authentic selves. We can Educate & Rejuvenate together by becoming observers, choosing our directions, aligning ourselves, and supporting each other all along the way in utilizing the tools in this book.

I got a photo message from one of our members that touched my heart. It was a picture of two members of our community who traveled over an hour and a half to meet in person for lunch. They met through the Educate & Rejuvenate Club and have cultivated a lasting friendship that would never have happened had they not chosen to grow together in a group coaching setting.

While I'd love to be your coach beyond these pages and have you join our community, there's no single way to utilize these tools and foster an uplifting community. You can also Educate & Rejuvenate with a friend by sharing this book with a friend once you've completed it. As you both strive to apply these tools, you can share your journeys and lift each other when you have setbacks. Even better, bring together a group of friends and do a book club to discuss what you each learned inside these pages to gain an even deeper understanding and learn from each other.

However you decide to find your community, I recommend finding one because when we come together, we are stronger than we could ever be alone. While our journeys are unique, we also have so much in common. We all have negative thoughts, feel emotions, and sometimes are dysregulated or people-pleasing. It's part of our shared humanity.

But we want to be mindful of the type of social circles we cultivate, because who we surround ourselves with shapes who we become. David McLellan of Harvard University closely studied high achievers for 25 years. He found that the most essential factor determining their success was their "reference group," meaning the people they spend the most time with (Monasterio, 2014). This makes sense because, as we learned earlier in this book, we naturally want to "fit in" with those around us.

We could use this knowledge to our advantage by creating a circle of support with fellow educators who are striving to become self-aware, consciously choosing what they want in their lives, and aligning themselves to it. When we come together and grow together, it makes our transformation even more impactful. As we surround ourselves with like-hearted educators who also want to see a transformation in their lives, we shape each other's experiences.

Coming together as a community is one of the most substantial ways to help you improve your comeback rate, as you aren't just creating a shift in your identity as someone who keeps promises to yourself. You're joining a group of people doing it right along with you.

Together, we refuse to become victims of the struggles that arise as we teach but use them as opportunities to rise stronger. We will cheer on another educator's wins as if they were our own. Instead of using another's triumph to feel bad about ourselves, we see their progress as inspiration for what's possible. No matter what comes our way, we have a soft place to land where we can share our misguided thoughts, worst fears, and perspectives without shame or judgment, only love.

Conclusion
Your Educate & Rejuvenate Transformation Begins Now

I recently came across a heartfelt post in a large teacher Facebook group. A fellow educator bravely shared her struggle with what she called "burnout guilt," expressing a sense of inadequacy for not keeping up with the exhaustive pace of her past. The comments poured in on this post, with many teachers saying they felt the exact same way.

I wish I'd saved the post to see this teacher's update. (If I could find that post again, I would send her a copy of this book!) But one thing remained clear from the post—this teacher was not alone. I've seen similar posts in many other teacher and homeschool Facebook groups, that education is a pursuit of either doing everything and feeling burned out or not doing everything but feeling bad about it.

As you read this book's final pages, I hope it becomes clear that living in these extremes is not a requirement. You don't have to be the teacher in a puddle of tears on the floor after losing a library book, as I was when I was student teaching.

In the quiet echoes of lost library books and tear-stained classroom floors, I discovered a truth that echoes through the hearts of educators everywhere: the journey to reignite our passion and thrive as teachers begins from within and expands as we connect with other educators with similar goals. In this book, we've unveiled a three-step guide to transform your teaching, renew your spirit, and rekindle the flame within. This isn't just a book; it's a lifeline for educators navigating the challenges of today's educational landscape.

First, you learned how to **Observe Yourself,** where we learned how to tap into self-awareness with curiosity and self-compassion. We want to observe our thoughts because they ultimately shape our feelings, actions, and results. It's not the circumstances of our lives, but our perception that shapes our experiences. We'll need to learn how to see through our cultured programming and cognitive distortions to challenge and alter these thoughts while staying true to ourselves.

We also learned that we naturally tend to resist, avoid, or react to our emotions. We do this to try to get out of feeling the emotion, but feelings buried alive don't just go away. Instead, we can observe them and process through them by naming them, breathing into them, and noticing where we feel them in our bodies. Meditation can also be a powerful way to get us into the present moment and move through our emotions.

There are also times our nervous system is dysregulated, meaning we are stuck in stress, and we'll need to complete the stress cycle first and foremost. To regulate ourselves, physical activity (movement) is the best way because of our body's instinct to get away from the stress. Breathing exercises, connecting with others, affection, laughter, crying, and creative expression can also help.

After self-observation, it's time to **Choose Your Direction**. Many of us don't know what we truly want and overoook our true desires amidst the busyness of teaching and all the other roles in our lives and the desire to please everyone. In our pursuit of love and connection, we often prioritize external validation over understanding our needs and embracing our true authentic selves.

We don't realize it, but we utilize people-pleasing as a mechanism to alleviate our own concerns rather than genuinely serving others. Unspoken expectations and the quest for love tied to specific expressions lead to a lack of true connection when we abandon our genuine selves.

After we get clear on our own needs, we can start to think more consciously. As we've learned, our selective attention is trained to prove our thoughts right, so as we think new, believable thoughts we can retrain it to work for us rather than against us. We can also set and create goals for ourselves from the mindset of abundance. They can be a powerful tool to help us challenge our thinking and overcome our mindset blocks. As we change our thinking, we'll feel differently which will make it easier to take actions that will reach our goals. Reaching our goals doesn't make us a better person, but they reveal what we've already had the capacity to do all along and get us where we want to be.

Once we've observed ourselves and chosen our direction, we want to **Align Ourselves** by navigating our chosen path with the guidance of our inner compass. The quest for a perfect teacher-life balance often overlooks the crucial element of alignment: choosing what truly matters and letting go of the rest, driven by a clear sense of purpose.

To stay aligned, consider creating a vision board, keeping goals in sight daily. Establishing morning and evening routines cultivates habits that keep you connected with yourself while also staying focused on your objectives. Creating and honoring boundaries out of love ensures we protect our physical, mental, and emotional health while maintaining relationships with others.

We can also keep alignment in mind as we create our schedules by making sure we make space for both urgent tasks and those that are important long term, while delegating and deleting other tasks. Creating an "ideal week" template is helpful so we aren't starting from scratch with weekly planning (inside and outside of teaching). By spending just an hour creating our schedule and calendar each week, we can make sure the important things are done while clearing our mental space.

Whether with our schedule, our goals, our thoughts, or feelings, we will experience setbacks. It is all part of the journey. But we will see improvements in our ability to become self aware and choose to align ourselves again. Our ability to bounce back from these challenges is crucial for forward motion. We'll get faster and it'll start to flow more naturally.

Every baby step along the way is a cause for celebration. Remember to look at how far you've come rather than constantly moving the goal post to "when" you will be happy. You can celebrate right now as you finish up this book- which is a huge accomplishment! As we focus on one percent improvement and owning our wins, over time they will add up and we will see transformational growth.

As we embrace the transformative power of self-awareness, conscious choices, and alignment, let this journey be a testament that, like a phoenix rising from the ashes, you too can soar beyond the constraints of stress, overwhelm, and burnout. Educate & Rejuvenate isn't just a philosophy; it's your ticket to a thriving, passionate, and fulfilling life as an educator and beyond. This final chapter isn't an end; it's a new beginning—a promise to yourself that you're worth the investment of time and self-love, and through this journey, you will emerge not just as an empowered teacher but as a rejuvenated soul shaking off the ashes of burnout that have held you down.

Closing the book is not the end; it's a call to action. As you embark on this transformative journey, remember that the impact of a rejuvenated teacher extends far beyond the confines of the classroom. In choosing to Educate & Rejuvenate, you're not just investing in yourself but in the countless lives you touch each day. Picture a ripple effect spreading through the educational landscape, touching students, colleagues, and the community at large. It's a movement, a revolution fueled by the collective power of teachers of all kinds who refuse to settle for a life of mere survival.

This isn't only a framework that will shape your teaching, but your entire life, and the ripple effect will impact everyone around you. Many of the educators I've seen naturally find themselves teaching these skills to their students and/or their own children and helping them shape their own positive self-talk, process their feelings, and regulate themselves. You will likely see this, too. This expansion will touch the hearts and minds and increase your contribution wherever you are. And it's not that you are becoming a better person than you were before; you're simply unveiling what has always been within you.

Throughout your teaching journey, let the threads of self-awareness, conscious choices, and alignment weave a story of resilience, purpose, and unwavering passion. The road ahead may present challenges, setbacks, and moments of doubt, but with the tools from this book at your fingertips, you are ready for whatever comes your way.

As you turn the last page, remember that this isn't goodbye but a 'see you later'—a commitment to **educating _and_ rejuvenating,** from here on out. You don't have to go at it alone, in fact, you'll be even more successful if you join other educators who are doing the same. Here are some ways you can continue this process with our Educate & Rejuvenate community:

- Tune in to the weekly Educate & Rejuvenate Podcast (listen on Apple or Spotify or watch on YouTube) and discuss with fellow educators in the free Educated & Rejuvenated Collective Facebook group.
- Sign up for our next Educate & Rejuvenate Virtual Conference
- For even more support, you can join me in the Educate & Rejuvenate Club, where you'll likely be able to hop on a call

with me and a group of supportive educators in less than a week!

Whatever you choose, when we come together with other educators as a community through this process, we become unstoppable. Embrace your journey, celebrate the wins, and learn from the setbacks. Share your experiences, insights, and newfound wisdom with fellow educators. I'd love to hear them too!

Drop me a message at hello@educateandrejuvenate.com, post an update in the Facebook group, or shoot me a DM on Instagram @educateandrejuvenate.

Let this be the beginning of a new chapter for you—a chapter where 'Educate & Rejuvenate' isn't just a title on a bookshelf but a mantra that echoes in your heart. Thank you for allowing me to be a part of your transformative journey. I can't wait to see you in the free Facebook group or at our Educate & Rejuvenate event! The journey is just beginning.

Together, let us redefine the narrative of teaching, one rejuvenated soul at a time. I can't wait to hear more of the story, and I'll be cheering you on, always!

With love and gratitude,

Acknowledgements

If you had told me ten years ago that I would write a self-help book for educators, I would have thought you were crazy. Yet here we are, and as I write we are just months away from this book reaching your hands. The process of translating the concepts I teach as a life coach into written words has been an experience of learning and growth, and my true motivation was to share these messages with you, the reader.

While the journey of writing this book was often a solitary endeavor—staring at a blank screen with writer's block, watching the sun rise as I plugged along writing, burning the midnight oil, or catching a spark of inspiration on my notes app while running errands—it wouldn't be in your hands today without the invaluable support of others. For that, I want to express my deepest gratitude. First and foremost, I would like to thank my incredible husband, Randy Sorenson, who has been unwaveringly supportive of my pursuit of writing this book. His continuous support with our kids and homeschooling–and even encouraging me to go on "book writing" getaways while he held down the fort at home–helped bring this book to life. He also helped me discover the title of this book during our discussion on a road trip. He was also there to listen when I got frustrated with writer's block (and even made me a "writers block" pencil holder). Love you forever, babe.

I'd also like to thank my three beautiful children–Parker, Brielle, and Peter, for the opportunity I have to be your teacher and mom. You have always been a source of inspiration, and I've loved your interest and support as I wrote this book, bringing you along in the process. Thank you for helping me "get out of my head" with fun dance and field trip breaks. To my sister (and fellow author), Victoria La Rue, Thank you for your writing insight and tips as I was on my writing journey. To my parents- Kristine & Dan Cox, and Loren & April Jorgensen, sister Rachel Jorgensen, and my in-laws Kelly & Deena Sorenson (plus all extended family members) I couldn't have done it without your love and support of this endeavor.

Thank you to the TeacherGoals Publishing team for bringing this book to the world. Brad Weinstein, thank you for believing in me and encouraging me to sign the contract and write this book. Alaina Clark-Weinstein, your support throughout the writing process has been invaluable. To the incredible editors—John Wick, Carrie Turner, and Kate Allyson—you turned my words into gold (and reduced my usual wordiness!). Tricia Fuglestad, thank you for creating the beautiful cover design. Heather Brown and Aubrey Labitigan for formatting. Lisa Dunnigan, thank you for connecting me with the TeacherGoals team.

I couldn't have made the time to write this book without the support of my incredible team at Educate & Rejuvenate (formerly Wife Teacher Mommy). Thank you to Rachael Kimball for proofreading the initial draft. Thank you to Kelcie Thomas, Kinsey Cornaby, Megan Osborn, and Emily Rasi-Koskinen for your day-to-day work. It wouldn't have been possible without you! I also want to thank former team members Karel Dimalanta and Boone Hogg for their contributions during the earlier phases of the book writing process, as well as all past Wife Teacher Mommy

Acknowledgements

team members for helping the company become what it is today. Chrissy Nichols, as our first life coach to join our team in the Club, you have been an example to me and brought so much goodness to my life and has been a support and a light on my journey to becoming a coach. I'd also love to thank Bonnie Wiscome, Kamee Bisson and Fracini Estes for their coaching contributions and perspectives in the Club, as listening to their calls have helped me find some more common themes for the book.

Lizzie Langston, my first life coach, taught me the power of the self-coaching model and the mind-body connection. I appreciate your support, feedback, and coaching as I wrote this book. This book, and the framework itself, was possible because I could bounce ideas off you—such a full-circle moment. Whether through 1:1 coaching or with group programs, thank you to the many coaches who have paved the way for me to become a coach myself. Brooke Castillo and her team at The Life Coach School for their certificate program. My business coach Kara Charron inspired me to start the Club, grow my teams and bring about the Educate & Rejuvenate events. Michelle Arant and Kris Plachy for the introduction to growing a business and team. Jody Moore for the many things I've learned in your program over the years. Lindsay Poelman for the growth and expansion I've had from your program, and lastly Bev Aron for the transformations I've seen in my life from your monthly learning topics for coaches. A special shout out to my friends Brooke Snow, Karlee Phelps, and Megan Lloyd who I met through a book club and encouraged me and supported me during some of the emotional toll that came from this process. To my long-haul business besties who have been along with me on my journey in business, life, and writing this book- Emily Van Natter Stephenson, Heidi

Van Natter, Teresa Kwant, Kirsten Tulsian, Cassie Tabrizi, Jacqueline Ortiz, Amy Neilsen, Faith Joy Solum, and so many more. For any work friends who I may have neglected to mention here, please know that I love and appreciate you, too. Kristina Kuzmic, thank you for the hope and humor you provided to our Educate & Rejuvenate community and the inspiration you've been to write my own book. Gabrielle Bernstein, thank you for showing me how to have less fear and more faith as this book is put out into the universe. Jamie Kern Lima, thank you for sharing your stories reminding me that I can believe in myself no matter how hard it gets, and I am inherently worthy no matter what.

Our Educate & Rejuvenate Club members are always a source of inspiration to me. I learn as much from you as you do from me, and I cherish every moment I get to spend coaching you. And to every educator who has participated in one of our events, listened to the Educate & Rejuvenate podcast, or shared about this work with a friend- thank you for making what I do here at Educate & Rejuvenate possible, including writing this book. I love what I do and am grateful to be connected to such an incredible community.

About the Author

Kelsey Sorenson is a former third-grade teacher and substitute teacher turned homeschool mom, certified life coach, and author. As the founder of **Educate & Rejuvenate**, her work has been spotlighted on platforms like *We Are Teachers, Teachers Pay Teachers, Show Up For Teachers, Teach Your Heart Out,* and *The Deseret News*. Kelsey and her team have empowered hundreds of thousands of educators to streamline their planning, find balance in their multifaceted lives, and reignite their passion for teaching through her **Educate & Rejuvenate Club**, **Educate & Rejuvenate Conferences**, time-saving resources, and her Amazon #1 Bestseller, *Educate & Rejuvenate: A 3-Step Guide to Revitalize Your Teaching, Renew Your Spirit, and Reignite Your Passion for Life*. She also hosts *Educate & Rejuvenate: The Podcast*. A proud "Swiftie," Kelsey can often be found with a Taylor Swift song playing and a Coke Zero in hand—when she's not tuning into a podcast or audiobook, spending time with her husband and 3 children, or enjoying yoga and strength training.

DON'T FORGET to claim your Educate & Rejuvenate resources! With your book purchase, you can download a beautiful PDF workbook to allow you to apply everything you've learned. Plus, you'll get exclusive reader-only video training and coaching to go along with it to learn on-the-go inside the Educate & Rejuvenate mobile app.

Join Our Educate & Rejuvenate Club

Ready to take your journey to the next level and work directly with Kelsey to apply everything you've learned from the book and so much more? By joining our Educate & Rejuvenate Club, you'll unlock:

Live Coaching Calls & Replays–Get inspired and rejuvenated with real-time guidance and access to previous sessions.

In-Depth Trainings Library–Dive deeper into the concepts from this book and beyond, with comprehensive resources designed to enhance your teaching and well-being.

Thousands of Printable Resources–Save time and enrich your teaching experience with our extensive collection of handy, printable materials.

VIP Access to Virtual Conferences–Join our exclusive Educate & Rejuvenate conferences and connect with fellow educators in a vibrant, supportive environment.

On-the-Go App Access–Keep coaching tips and teaching ideas right at your fingertips, wherever you go.

A Supportive Community–Connect with a group of like-hearted educators who truly understand and uplift you throughout the year.

It's an incredible value at an unbeatable price. Investing in yourself means investing in your success, happiness, and growth. Don't miss out—learn more about how to join us and elevate your Educate & Rejuvenate journey! Visit www.teachergoals.com/rejuvenate-club or scan the QR code!

> *Coaching is so valuable and makes me feel that I'm not alone in my stressful life situations. I love supporting and learning from fellow teachers. They say it takes a village to raise a child, but this is also true of being a teacher! My village is the Educate & Rejuvenate community.*
> -Sarah Snider

Bibliography

Introduction:

Marken, S., & Agrawal, S. (2022, September 13). *K-12 Workers Have Highest Burnout Rate in U.S.* Gallup. Retrieved April 24, 2024, from https://news.gallup.com/poll/393500/workers-highest-burnout-rate.aspx

Chapter One:

Self-Compassion book- Neff, K. (2011). *Self-Compassion* (pp. 41-42). William Morrow.

Sikhism: The concept of "Sarbat da Bhala" translates to the well-being of all and reflects a commitment to the welfare of the entire human race.

Chapter Two:

Schorling, J. (2024, March 4). *The Space Between Stimulus And Response.* University of Virginia. Retrieved April 24, 2024, from https://news.med.virginia.edu/mindfulness/2024/03/04/the-space-between-stimulus-and-response/

Frankl, V. E. (2006). *Man's Search for Meaning* (6th ed., p. 66). Beacon Press, Boston.

Augustine, Z. G. (2017, March 24). *"You have power over your mind — Not outside events. Realize this and you will find strength.".* Medium. Retrieved April 24, 2024, from https://medium.com/@zga/you-have-power-over-your-mind-not-outside-events-realize-this-and-you-will-find-strength-f17f75f03180

Rose, K. (2024). *Epictetus on How to Live a Good, Fulfilling Life.* The Inward Turn. Retrieved April 24, 2024,from https://theinwardturn.com/epictetus-on-how-to-live-a-good-fulfilling-life/ In text- (Rose, 2024)

Fletcher, K. (2024). *200+ Wise Ralph Waldo Emerson Quotes.* Thought.is. Retrieved April 24, 2024, from https://

thought.is/ralph-waldo-emerson-quotes/ In text (Fletcher, 2024)

Beck, A. T., Rush, A. J., Shaw, B. F., & Emery, G. (1979). Cognitive Therapy of Depression. Guilford Press.

Judith Beck book- Beck, J. S. (2020). *Cognitive Behavior Therapy: Basics and Beyond* (3rd ed.). The Guilford Press.

Feeling Great book- Burns, D. D. (2020). *Cognitive Behavior Therapy: Basics and Beyond*. PESI Publishing & Media.

[Kristina Kuzmic]. (2017, December 28). *Things We Tell Ourselves* [Video]. YouTube. https://www.youtube.com/watch?v=PnzlG5NYT8M

Malkasian, K. (2022, January 31). *Stop "Shoulding" on Yourself!* Coral Reef Counseling. Retrieved April 24, 2024, from https://www.coralreefcounseling.com/post/stop-shoulding-on-yourself

100 Positive Mindfulness Quotes To Be Present In Life. (2024, April 18). *100 Positive Mindfulness Quotes To Be Present In Life*. Put The Kettle On. Retrieved April 24, 2024, from https://putthekettleon.ca/mindfulness-quotes/

Chapter Three:

Castillo, B. (2014, October 9). *The Self Coaching Model*. The Life Coach School. Retrieved April 24, 2024, from https://thelifecoachschool.com/podcast/26/ In text (Castillo, 2014).

Smith, S. (2023, September 8). *From the R Line to the F Line* [Conference Presentation]. The Life Coach School.

"Coaching for Primary Care Physician Well-being: A Randomized Trial and Follow-up Analysis"- McGonagle, A. K., Schwab, L., Yahanda, N., Duskey, H., Gertz, N., Prior, L., Roy, M., & Kriegel, G. (2020). Coaching for primary care physician well-being: A randomized trial and follow-up analysis. *Journal of occupational health psychology*, *25*(5), 297–314. https://doi.org/10.1037/ocp0000180

Chapter Four:

Vahrmeyer, M. (2021, April 21). *Unexpressed emotions will never die*. Brighton and Hove Psycotherapy. Retrieved April 24, 2024, from https://www.brightonandhovepsychotherapy.com/blog/unexpressed-emotions-will-never-die/

Lieberman, M. D., Eisenberger, N. I., Crockett, M. J., Tom, S. M., Pfeifer, J. H., & Way, B. M. (2007). Putting feelings into words: affect labeling disrupts amygdala activity in response to affective stimuli. *Psychological science, 18*(5), 421–428. https://doi.org/10.1111j.14679280.2007.01916.x

Siegel, D. J., & Bryson, T. P. (2011). *The Whole-Brain Child: Revolutionary Strategies to Nurture Your Child's Developing Mind*. Delacorte Press.

Brown, B. (2021). *Atlas of the Heart: Mapping Meaningful Connection and the Language of Human Experience*. Random House.

(Brown, 2021)

Nhất Hạnh, T. (1987). *Being Peace*. Parallax Press.

Nhất Hạnh, T. (1997). *Stepping into Freedom: An Introduction to Buddhist Monastic Training* (A. Laity, Trans.). Parallax Press.

Brach, T. (2000). *Radical Acceptance: Embracing Your Life With the Heart of a Buddha*. Bantam.

Dispenza, J. (2017). *Becoming Supernatural: How Common People are Doing the Uncommon*. Hay House.

Castillo, B. (2015, January 29). *Creating Emotion*. The Life Coach School. Retrieved April 25, 2024, from https://thelifecoachschool.com/podcast/42/

Chapter Five:

Vallie, S., & Juber, M., MD (2022, September 29). *Sympathetic Nervous System: What to Know*. Web MD. Retrieved April 25, 2024, from https://www.webmd.com/brain/sympathetic-nervous-system-what-to-knowNagoski, E., & Nagoski, A. (2020). *Burnout: The Secret to Unlocking the Stress Cycle* (2nd ed.). Penguin Random House Publishing Group.

Castillo, B. (2022, June 1). *Coach Certification Program* [Training for Certified Coaches]. thelifecoachschool.com

Sorensen, J. (n.d.). *Breath: The Remote Control of Your Nervous System and Brain*. Airway Stents. Retrieved April 25, 2024, from https://alaxousa.com/breath-the-remote-control-of-your-nervous-system-and-brain/

Johnson, L. E. (2020, October 23). *Here are 7 things Collin Kartchner said about how to #SavetheKids from social media*. Deseret News. Retrieved April 25, 2024, from https://www.deseret.com/entertainment/2020/10/23/21528803/collin-kartchner-death-save-the-kids-save-the-parents-utah-social-media-dangers/

Peterson, N. (2023, August 17). *The Benefits of Hugs*. Ridgecrest Herbals. Retrieved April 25, 2024, from https://rcherbals.com/blogs/herb-nerds/the-benefits-of-hugs

Escalante, A (2020, June 9). *Here's How Science Says You Can Give The Perfect Hug (Once Social Distancing Is Over)*. Forbes. Retrieved April 25, 2024, from https://www.forbes.com/sites/alisonescalante/2020/06/09/how-to-give-the-perfect-hug-according-to-science/

Taylor Swift's new album was a 'lifeline' for the pop superstar. (2024, February 19). Yahoo! News. Retrieved April 25, 2024, from https://news.yahoo.com/taylor-swifts-album-lifeline-pop-100000852.html

Wright, A., LMFT, & Sills, D. (2022, May 23). *What Is the Window of Tolerance, and Why Is It So Important?* Psychology Today. Retrieved April 25, 2024, from https://www.psychologytoday.com/us/blog/making-the-whole-beautiful/202205/what-is-the-window-tolerance-and-why-is-it-so-important

Levine, P., PhD, & Curlander, K., MA, LPC (2022, May 23). *The Inner Thoughts of a Trauma Guru*. Higher Practice Podcast. Retrieved April 25, 2024, from https://psychiatryinstitute.com/podcast/inner-thoughts-trauma-guru-dr-peter-levine-hpp-51/#:~:text=Psychological%20 trauma%20can%20happen%20to,ourselves%20safe%20 in%20a%20situation.

Fast Facts: Preventing Adverse Childhood Experiences. (2023, June 9). Centers for Disease Control and Prevention. Retrieved April 25, 2024, from https://www.cdc.gov/ violenceprevention/aces/fastfact.html

Barbash, E., Ph.D. (2023, March 17). *Different Types of Trauma: Small 't' versus Large 'T'*. Psycology Today. Retrieved April 28, 2024, from https://www.psychologytoday.com/us/ blog/trauma-and-hope/201703/different-types-trauma-small-t-versus-large-t

Poelman, L., & Sorenson, K. (2023, November 14). *What To Know About Trauma*. Wife Teacher Mommy, Educate & Rejuvenate. Retrieved April 25, 2024, from https://www. wifeteachermommy.com/podcast/trauma/

Van der Kolk, B. A. (2014). *The Body Keeps the Score: Brain, Mind, and Body in the Healing of Trauma*. Viking.

Davidson, L., & Sorenson, K. (2023, November 7). *Get To Know Your Nervous System*. Wife Teacher Mommy, Educate & Rejuvenate. Retrieved April 25, 2024, from https://www.wifeteachermommy.com/podcast/nervous-system/

Chapter 6:

Cassavetes, N. (2004). *The Notebook*. New Line Cinema.

Condition of Education (2023, May). *Characteristics of Public School Teachers*. National Center for Education Statistics. Retrieved April 25, 2024, from https://nces.ed.gov/ programs/coe/indicator/clr/public-school-teachers

Gómez-Baya, D., Lucia-Casademunt, A. M., & Salinas-Pérez, J. A. (2018). Gender Differences in Psychological Well-Being and Health Problems among European Health Professionals: Analysis of Psychological Basic Needs and Job Satisfaction. *International journal of environmental research and public health*, *15*(7), 1474. https://doi.

org/10.3390/ijerph15071474

Oppong, T. (2023, March 1). *Carl Jung — You Are Not What Happened to You*. Medium. Retrieved April 25, 2024, from https://medium.com/personal-growth/carl-jung-you-are-not-what-happened-to-you-9dc45bb93539

Maslow, A. H. (1943). *A Theory of Human Motivation*. Classics in the History of Psychology. Retrieved April 29, 2024, from https://psychclassics.yorku.ca/Maslow/motivation.htm

Lima, J. K. (2024). *Worthy*. Hay House.

Castillo, B. (2014, June 26). *The Manual*. The Life Coach School. Retrieved April 25, 2024, from https://thelifecoachschool.com/podcast/11/

Brown, B. (2021). *Atlas of the Heart: Mapping Meaningful Connection and the Language of Human Experience*. Random House.

(Brown, 2021)

Cyrus, Miley. "Flowers." *Endless Summer Vacation*, Columbia Records, 2023

Nichols, C. 2023. *Coaching Call*. The Chrissy Concept. Retrieved April 25, 2024, from https://www.thechrissyconcept.com/

Chapter 7:

Tarvis, C., & Aronson, E. (2020). *Mistakes Were Made (but Not By Me)* (2nd ed.). Mariner Books.

Liptack, A. (2014, December 22). *Supreme Court Justices Admit Inconsistency, and Embrace It*. The New York Times. Retrieved April 25, 2024, from https://www.nytimes.com/2014/12/23/us/supreme-court-justices-admit-inconsistency-and-embrace-it.html

Kukolic, S. (2017, November 18). *There Will Be Good Days And Bad Days*. HuffPost. Retrieved April 25, 2024, from https://www.huffpost.com/entry/post_b_13050682

Chapter 8:

Hardy, B. (2022). *Be Your Future Self Now*. Hay House Business.

Sullivan, D., & Hardy, B. (2021). *The Gap and The Gain*. Hay House Business.

Italian Renaissance Masters: Botticelli, Leonardo da Vinci, Raphael, and Michelangelo. (2020, November 6). Smithsonian Associates. Retrieved April 25, 2024, from https://smithsonianassociates.org/ticketing/tickets/italian-renaissance-masters-botticelli-leonardo-da-vinci-raphael-and-michelangelo

Clear, J. (2018). *Atomic Habits*. Avery.

Bernstein, G. (2019). *The Universe Has Your Back: Transform Fear to Faith*. Hay House.

Chapter 9:

Arguinchona, J. H., & Tadi, P. (2023, July 24). *Neuroanatomy, Reticular Activating System*. National Library of Medicine. Retrieved April 25, 2024, from https://www.ncbi.nlm.nih.gov/books/NBK549835/

Clear, J. (2018). *Atomic Habits*. Avery.

Chapter 10:

Kuzmic, K. (2020). *Hold On, But Don't Hold Still*. Viking.

Eisenhower, D. D. (1954, August 19). *Address at the Second Assembly of the World Council of Churches, Evanston, Illinois*. The American Presidency Project. Retrieved April 25, 2024, from https://www.presidency.ucsb.edu/documents/address-the-second-assembly-the-world-council-churches-evanston-illinois

Covey, S. R. (2004). *The 7 Habits of Highly Effective People: Powerful Lessons in Personal Change*. Free Press.

[PBS News Hour]. Obama, M. (2016, March 8). *Watch Michelle Obama speak on International Women's Day* [Video]. YouTube. https://www.youtube.com/watch?v=FIN1F0TyadM

Chapter 11:

[NowThis Impact]. (2022, October 30). *Dancer Captivates Audience With 'Staircase' Routine* [Video]. YouTube. https://www.youtube.com/watch?v=WrY22UROOUU

Bernstein, G. (2019). *The Universe Has Your Back: Transform Fear to Faith*. Hay House.

[Nysmuseum]. (2014, January 20). *Dr. Martin Luther King, Jr.'s 1962 Speech in NYC* [Video]. YouTube. https://www.youtube.com/watch?v=k7t35qDYHgc

Klug, L., & Bernstein, G. (2016, August 30). *Life got you down? There's a catchphrase for that*. The Times of Israel. Retrieved April 25, 2024, from https://www.timesofisrael.com/life-got-you-down-theres-a-catchphrase-for-that/

Clear, J. (2018). *Atomic Habits*. Avery.

Sullivan, D., & Hardy, B. (2021). *The Gap and The Gain*. Hay House Business.

Hunt, B. (Writer), Sudeikis, J. (Writer), Kelly, J. (Writer), Delaney, M. (Director), 2020 October 2. The Hope That Kills You. (Season 1, Episode 10). In B. Lawrence, J. Sudeikis, J. Ingold, B. Wrubel. *Ted Lasso*. Apple TV+

Mann, A., MD, Shah, A. N., MD, Thibodeau, P. S., PhD, MSW, LCSW, Dyrbye, L., MD, MHPE, Syed, A., BS, Woodward, M. A., MD, MSc, Thurmon, K., MD, MPH, Jones, C. D., MD, MS, Dunbar, K. S., MD, & Fainstad, T., MD (2023, October 4). *Online Well-Being Group Coaching Program for Women Physician Trainees A Randomized Clinical Trial*. JAMA Network. Retrieved April 25, 2024, from https://jamanetwork.com/journals/jamanetworkopen/fullarticle/2810135

Monasterio, J. (2014, July 21). *Surround yourself with like minded people to become the person you strive to be*. Wise With Age. Retrieved April 25, 2024, from https://wiserwithage.com/2014/07/21/surround-yourself-with-like-minded-people-to-become-the-person-you-strive-to-be/

More From TeacherGoals

The Science of Reading in Action
By Malia Holowell

This is not just a book. It's a teaching movement! With 67 % of U.S. kids not proficient in reading, according to 2022 data, the status quo isn't working.

This book tackles the main obstacles: training, tools and support offering:
- Evidence-based insights on teaching, reading, dispelling social media myths
- Solutions for common challenges facing struggling readers
- Ready-to-use activities and strategies that simplify brain-friendly reading instruction
- A method to help students memorize words 10x faster than with flashcards
- Techniques to ensure no student falls behind

Written by Malia Hollowell, a certified educator and Stanford alum, this book is your all-in-one guide for making reading instruction effective and engaging.

Body and Brain Brilliance
By Dr. Lori Desautels

Discover the transformative power of *Body and Brain Brilliance*. Navigate through today's unprecedented stress with essential neuro-educational tools. Empower adults and children to cultivate emotional resilience and social connection, fostering classrooms where everyone feels seen, heard, and understood.

Dive in, and embark on a journey of healing and comprehensive well-being.

Bulk Orders

TeacherGoals Publishing, LLC offers bulk orders for any of our titles. A minimum of 25 copies must be ordered for bulk orders, and orders qualify for discounts. You can also request information about signed copies, book studies, and more. Scan the QR code for more information.

Children's Books From TeacherGoals

EXPLORE THE ENTIRE MONSTERS HAVE MANNERS COLLECTION OF BOOKS, T-SHIRTS, STICKERS, AND A FREE 20-PAGE ACTIVITY PACKET AT TEACHERGOALS.COM OR SCAN THE QR CODE

BOOKS, SHIRTS, AR POSTERS, STICKERS, & MORE • TEACHERGOALS.COM

EXPLORE THE ENTIRE PETER O'METER COLLECTION OF BOOKS, T-SHIRTS, AR STICKERS, AR POSTERS AND A FREE 50-PAGE ACTIVITY PACKET AT TEACHERGOALS.COM OR SCAN THE QR CODE

www.ingramcontent.com/pod-product-compliance
Lightning Source LLC
LaVergne TN
LVHW011935070526
838202LV00054B/4663